NATIONALISM AND INTERNATIONAL SOCIETY

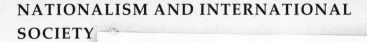

DATE DUE

Cambridge Studies in International Relations is a joint initiative of Cambridge University Press and the British International Studies Association (BISA). The series will include a wide range of material, from undergraduate textbooks and surveys to research-based monographs and collaborative volumes. The aim of the series is to publish the best new scholarship in International Studies from Europe, North America and the rest of the world.

D1167260

CAMBRIDGE STUDIES IN INTERNATIONAL RELATIONS

NATIONALISM AND INTERNATIONAL SOCIETY

JAMES MAYALL

Reader in International Relations, London School of Economics

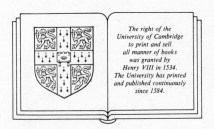

CAMBRIDGE UNIVERSITY PRESS

CAMBRIDGE

NEW YORK   PORT CHESTER

MELBOURNE   SYDNEY

Published by the Press Syndicate of the University of Cambridge
The Pitt Building, Trumpington Street, Cambridge CB2 1RP
40 West 20th Street, New York, NY 10011, USA
10 Stamford Road, Oakleigh, Melbourne 3166, Australia

First published 1990

Printed in Great Britain by Redwood Brown Ltd, Trowbridge, Wilts

British Library cataloguing in publication data
Mayall, James
Nationalism and international society. –
(Cambridge studies in international relations: 10)
1. Nationalism. International aspects
I. Title
320.5'4

Library of Congress cataloguing in publication data
Mayall, James.
Nationalism and international society / James Mayall.
    p.   cm. – (Cambridge studies in international
relations: 10)
ISBN 0–521–37312–3. – ISBN 0–521–38961–5 (pbk.)
1. Nationalism.   2. International agencies.
3. International relations.
4. International economic relations.
I. Title
II. Series.
JC311.M38   1990
341.26–dc20   89–7284   CIP

ISBN 0 521 37312 3 hard covers
ISBN 0 521 38961 5 paperback

CE

CONTENTS

ACKNOWLEDGEMENTS

I wish to record my gratitude to the secretarial staff of the International Relations Department and the Centre of International Studies at the London School of Economics, and particularly Pam Hodges and Margaret Bothwell, without whose help this book could not have been prepared for publication. I am also grateful to the Government Department of Dartmouth College, New Hampshire and the Centre for Political Studies at Jawarharlal Nehru University, New Delhi, for providing me with conditions which were conducive to my beginning the book in 1984 and completing it in 1988. An earlier version of Chapter 4 appeared in *Millennium*: *Journal of International Studies* (vol. 11, no. 2, Summer 1985). I am grateful to the editors for permission to reprint some of this material here.

My intellectual debts to friends and colleagues are great. For several years I have helped to run a Seminar on Nationalism at the London School of Economics with Anthony Smith, Percy Cohen and George Schopflin and I am grateful to them for having encouraged my interest in the subject and to all those who have contributed to the seminar, for helping me develop my ideas. The finished typescript was read by Harry Beran, John Charvet, Michael Donelan, Mervyn Frost, Robert Jackson, Peter Lyon and John Vincent, all of whom made valuable comments and suggestions. Over many years, I have also benefited greatly in discussing the various themes of the book with Dennis Austin, David Baldwin, Ebba Dohlman, Roger Holmes, Maurice Keens-Soper, Margot Light, Ian Lustick, Berry Mayall, Cornelia Navari, Aswini Ray, Gautam Sen, Philip Windsor and many others. Finally I should like to thank Avril who not only bore with my anxieties during the final stages of writing, but was my most searching and helpful critic. Neither she nor anybody else can be held responsible for my views.

INTRODUCTION

This book traces the implications for international society of the national idea. It seeks answers to three questions. What is meant by international society? On what normative principles is the idea of international society based? How has nationalist doctrine, and more broadly the national idea, influenced its evolution? Its focus is different from much of the recent literature on nationalism, which seeks to explain its rise as a consequence of social, economic or intellectual developments. The focus in this study is on the consequences of nationalism for international society. It is thus about the impact of one idea on the fate of another.

Of these two ideas, whose encounter has helped to shape the twentieth century, nationalism is likely to be more familiar to many readers than international society. The meaning of both terms, however, is contested, and it may be helpful to identify the sense in which I use them in this book.

Even the possibility of international society is often denied by those who regard the prevalence of conflict in international relations as proof that they are not governed by the minimal solidarity which is necessary to ensure social cohesion. The possibility of international society is also denied by those who insist that the state establishes the boundaries of both political organisation and social morality. On this view, any order in international relations arises merely from the prudential calculations of competitive powers. Their behaviour is not constrained by moral considerations with a universal appeal; nor does it signify a set of shared values. At best their regular interaction can be described as an international system.[1]

Those who employ the concept of international society point out that the global system of world politics is historically derived from the European states-system as it developed between the seventeenth and twentieth centuries. Despite their rivalries and wars, European sovereigns acknowledged moral constraints on their behaviour and shared certain values. Without them neither international law nor the devel-

1

opment of a diplomatic system would have been possible. Moreover, the fact that they regularly invoked the social ideal in relations amongst themselves – just as their successors invoke the idea of an international community – strongly suggests that the idea of a society in which the sum is greater than the parts, actually influences the behaviour of governments.[2]

International society is a society of states, not of people. To the extent that this statement requires qualification, for example, to take account of the universal acknowledgement of human rights or schemes of economic cooperation across international frontiers, it is largely a consequence of the substitution of popular for dynastic or prescriptive sovereignty under the impact of nationalist ideas.

Nationalism is an even more fiercely contested concept than international society. The basic problem arises because the political utility of the national idea is not matched by its analytical clarity. The difficulty lies in defining the nation itself. Is it one phenomenon or many?

Much effort is devoted in the literature to answering this question, and to distinguishing between various types and sub-types.[3] Linguistic, ethnic, and political criteria have all been proposed, separately and in various combinations. In some parts of the world, nationalism arose in conjunction with liberal constitutionalism and democratic government; in others it was a reaction to imperial conquest. In nineteenth-century Europe claims for national self-determination were advanced in the name of allegedly pre-existing cultural communities. In twentieth-century Asia and Africa nationalist movements were more often political coalitions designed to fight colonialism. Only after independence did anti-colonial leaders face the task of building a nation to inhabit the state they had inherited. Finally, there are some communities whose national identity has been preserved for centuries, although they lack a political organisation and are dispersed in many different states.

In this book I have deliberately not sought to impose a single definition on the nation or on nationalism. This is not because I consider the substantive characteristics of different kinds of nationalism to be unimportant. Rather, it is because my concern is with the interaction of the ideas of nation and international society. From a sociological or historical standpoint, there are clearly many kinds of nationalism, but the national idea itself is not unclear. It holds that the world is (or should be) divided into nations and that the nation is the only proper basis for a sovereign state and the ultimate source of governmental authority. Where I refer to particular distinctions, as for

2

example between the mainly centralised nation-states of the industrial west and the state-nations of the third world, it is because these respective manifestations of the national idea have had a differential impact on the evolution and organisation of international society.

The argument itself falls into five parts. The first two chapters are concerned with theoretical questions. They deal initially – for reasons which flow from the book's main purpose – with the international context rather than, as in most books on nationalism, the nation itself. And because the central issue in the debate between the exponents of an international society, and their opponents, concerns the possibility of moral (or at least normative) constraints on state behaviour, the book opens with a brief discussion of the problems of grounding any theoretical account of international relations. Chief amongst these problems is the identity of the object of theory, namely international society. As a historical conception, however, its identity is not in doubt. Moreover, it is this historical conception which was challenged and then modified by nationalism, first in Europe and then world-wide. The process of challenge and accommodation between the ideas of nationalism and international society dictate the strategy of the rest of the book. Chapters 3 and 4 describe how, under the guise of the doctrine of self-determination and anti-colonialism, nationalism has created new states and pushed the boundaries of international society horizontally outwards, so that it is now co-extensive with the globe.

The enlargement of international society through the creation of new states followed a period in which the world had been integrated economically to an unprecedented degree. This was in part a consequence of successive waves of European imperial expansion from the fifteenth century onwards, and in part, of the development of an increasingly complex division of labour between the major industrial powers in the nineteenth and twentieth centuries. The emergence of a single world economy was accompanied by the development of a powerful liberal ideology which purported to explain the process. This ideology in turn provoked a nationalist reaction. Chapters 5 and 6 examine the confrontation between nationalist and liberal ideas about international economic relations and the resulting extension of state activity downwards into the lives of ordinary people and outwards into the management of the international economy.

After 1919 the idea of international society had been realised in institutional form by the provision of a framework for multilateral diplomacy, the League of Nations. After 1945, in addition to the United Nations, the successor organisation to the League, the idea was elaborated further by the establishment of an institutional frame-

3

work for economic cooperation. The nationalism of many post-colonial states was developed in reaction to this postwar international economic order. Chapters 7 and 8 discuss the reasons why economic development became such an important ingredient in third world nationalism, and the largely unsuccessful attempts of the third world states to alter the economic arrangements of international society in their favour. A short conclusion recapitulates the argument and reflects on its implications for the future.

1 THE SEARCH FOR THE INTERNATIONAL SYSTEM: THE PROBLEM OF THEORY

Everyone agrees that nationalism has had an enormous influence on international politics in the twentieth century. Whether this influence is to be regarded as benign or as a malignant growth, or whether it is merely a neutral fact, a datum which must be accepted before sensible political analysis can begin, is a more contentious question. All three positions have their adherents but they agree on little else than that national sentiment is pervasive and central to an understanding of the modern world.

For those who would like to construct a general theory of nationalism, the virtual absence of an authoritative account of its international impact is doubly regrettable.[1] On the one hand, without such an account, nationalism itself will continue to resist ultimate explanation, since it will not be clear how far it springs from, or is constrained by, a particular kind of international environment. On the other hand, in the analysis of international politics, nationalism is likely to be regarded as a convenient black box into which whatever cannot be explained in any other way – and in the literature this has always been a great deal – can be filed away without further consideration. But, regrettable or not, the absence of an authoritative account will not be easily overcome. The reason for this can be illustrated by comparing the impact of nationalism on the politics of individual states, with its impact on the system of states in general. In the first case, we can give a plausible account of the way in which nationalist ideas, and nationalist movements, first attacked and then conquered the doctrines of legitimacy and the institutions which supported the *ancien régime* in Europe, and the Asian and African empires of the European great powers. Many historians, sociologists and political scientists have done just this.[2] In the second case it is not entirely clear what we are talking about.

At first sight this judgement may seem unduly harsh. After all, those who have studied the origins and diffusion of nationalism are seldom in agreement on either its causes or its consequences for the modern state. Indeed the concept of the state itself is far from uncontroversial. Is it a sufficient, or merely a necessary condition that there should be a monopoly of legal force in the hands of the government, or that the government should have an ability to raise the necessary taxation to finance its activities, or that the independent existence of the state should be recognised by its peers? Should we accept the positive criteria that such questions imply, and adopt a purely descriptive definition of the state? If we adopt this position we will be led also to the conclusion that there are currently 159 states in the world because there are, undeniably, 159 members of the United Nations.

Or, should we accept (indeed, do we already secretly believe, whatever we say in public to the contrary) that in the final analysis only some states deserve to be taken seriously. On this view, just as in the fairy story, there are hidden criteria for telling a 'real' princess from a false one, so in the political world some states must be recognised as authentic, while the recognition that we give to others is either provisional or merely a matter of form. In the one case, the criteria have something to do with the sensitivity of a princess's skin to the pressure of a single pea felt through a great number of feather mattresses; in the other, the criteria are derived from the self-conscious understanding of a particular people about its special role in the collective destiny of mankind. The criteria in the fairy story are different from those in the political theory, but the principle is the same: there is a world of appearances, but there is, lying behind the formal and superficial order, also the 'real' thing.

This debate may seem trivial but it is not. Indeed, it encapsulates the two major positions in modern thought, the one insisting, in this case as in all others, that there must be unprivileged context-free standards of measurement and assessment if we are ever to be able to distinguish the known and knowable world from the world of fantasy and imagination; the other insisting, with equal power and possibly greater insight, that, whatever may be the case with regard to our understanding of the natural world, in human relations, that is in the world of culture, everything worth knowing is saturated with specific meanings and significances. There is no context-free knowledge: we either understand our own history in terms of its particular meaning to us, or we have no understanding of how we stand in relation to the past, and more importantly, to the future. The positivist idea of a scientific history – one which is governed by laws which operate independently of human will – is absurd. There is no significant distinction to be drawn between the impact of nationalism on the state and on international politics: the only interesting discussion is that which concerns the self-conscious development, abroad as well as at home, of 'real' historical nation-states.

But while this debate between positivists and historicists is central to an understanding of the modern world, it is also the kind of debate which does not hold out the possibility of unambiguous resolution. Moreover, the fact that historicists concede that there is an empirical world of states, as well as an historical world of 'real' states, establishes the context within which the analysis of nationalism can be located. And, in a world which seems increasingly shifting and uncertain, this relatively firm ground is comforting. At this stage, we can afford to be agnostic on the positivist/historicist issue. For present purposes it is sufficient to accept the formal order of the system of states.

The important point to note is that all these formal states, whose governments take part in the ritual quadrille of international diplomacy and enjoy the dignity of mutual recognition and membership of the United Nations, actually exist: they can be located on the map; they have more or less defined boundaries; they have settled populations and identifiable social and political institutions. Admittedly, as one consequence of nationalist politics and ideology, travelling from some parts of the world to other parts is an increasingly hazardous activity, but, if necessary, given determination, it can still be done. And because states are accessible in this way, their political systems are open to investigation, in principle if not always in fact.

By contrast, the international system has none of these properties. It has no concrete physical existence; its boundaries cannot be demarcated even in principle – what *on earth* could lie beyond the boundaries of the international political system – and one certainly cannot go there. Anyone who has ever tried to discuss the general context of international relations has been forced, sooner or later, to use some collective noun. Some have opted for the idea of a community of mankind, others for a society of states, yet others for a states-system, or world society, or a series of international regimes. Whatever collective noun is posited its purpose is to impose a degree of order on an area of human activity from which there is no escape but which is also notoriously anarchic. International relations are more often governed by contingency than by systematic rule-bound behaviour. Or so runs the familiar argument. But *posit* is the operative word. No wonder that since it lacks, even in a formal sense, any empirical content, the 'international system' has always been amongst the most contested ideas in the study of international relations.

7

It is because states exist within a wider world that an analysis of the impact of nationalism on international relations must start, not with the nation, but with an account of the prevailing conception of international society at the time of the rise of nationalism as a major force in world politics. Chapter 2 contains an account of this kind.

The argument is that although the problems of international relations raise major theoretical, indeed ultimately philosophical, questions, they cannot be understood from a purely theoretical standpoint. Before we can begin to evaluate the impact of nationalism on international politics, therefore, we need to look at this putative but disputed system as it developed in the pre-nationalist era.

THE SYSTEM IN QUESTION

In most disputes about the mapping of international politics, the major contending positions can be loosely described as Marxist, liberal and realist, even though some of the protagonists probably do not recognise their own ancestry and both Marx and the liberal founding fathers would certainly have wished to disinherit many of their progeny. I shall return to their arguments in other chapters of this book. For the moment, I shall set them aside, in the first case, because Marx did not have a conception of a legitimate international system or society; in the second, because although the early liberals did have such a conception – the idea of a cosmopolitan commercial society – in its residual political aspects, classical liberalism accepted many of the tenets of traditional European state theory.

It is with this theoretical tradition, with its roots in the world of medieval Christendom and antiquity, that we must first contend. The dominant although often implicit debate about the nature of the international system has always been between theorists of the state who saw themselves as political realists. The tradition of political realism, however, has its own embattled positions – let us call them the hard and soft versions of the argument. Essentially the distinction depends on the nature of the constraints that are accepted on the exercise of state power.

Students of international relations have seldom been noted for their hermneutic sensitivity. Like fundamentalist preachers, they have tended to plunder the major works of western political thought for texts which seem to illustrate one or other aspect of human nature or behaviour. In this way, despite the 2,000 years that separate them, Thucydides and Hobbes are frequently called to the same stand, to bear witness to and dignify the realist case. In the Melian debate

Thucydides has his Athenian generals underline the tragic consequences of the realist vision, namely that 'they that have the odds of power exact as much as they can, and the weak yield to such conditions as they can get'.[3] However, it is Hobbes, writing in the defence of the absolutist state, whose explanation of the fundamental nature of international relations is most often quoted by hard-line realists. In chapter 13 of the *Leviathan* he writes that:

> though there had never been any time, wherein particular men were in a condition of war one against another; yet in all times kings, and persons of sovereign authority, because of their independency, are in continual jealousies, and in the state and posture of gladiators, having their weapons pointing and their eyes fixed on one another; that is their forts, garrisons and guns upon the frontiers of their kingdoms; and continual spies upon their neighbours; which is a posture of war. But because they uphold, thereby, the industry of their subjects there does not follow from it that misery which accompanies the liberty of particular men.[4]

The image of the world generated by these texts is relentless and forbidding. It is an image of international politics as a state of war, in which, when the rhetoric of political discourse has been stripped away, power arbitrates. David Hume rightly doubted 'whether such a condition of human nature could ever exist, or if it did, could continue so long as to merit the appelation of a State'. But he also developed the logic of the realist image by adding that 'if such a state of mutual war and violence was ever real, the suspension of all laws of justice, from their absolute uncertainty, is a necessary and infallible consequence'.[5] In such a world the only constraints in the collective war of all against all arise from calculations about the strength of one's opponents and consequently from considerations of prudence. In such a world, moreover, the only *conceivable* over-arching inter-state system or order, would have been one which was, so to speak, 'built-in'. For example, it might be possible to imagine a principle of equilibrium such that the powers would hold one another in check regardless of intention or will.

In Europe, this was, indeed, one view of the working of the classical eighteenth-century balance of power. However, judging from the behaviour of governments who were intent on establishing their freedom of action, it was even then a view which was less likely to recommend itself to practical men of affairs than to intellectuals. Politicians like to believe that what they do makes a difference. But even if we accept that there is a principle of equilibrium in nature, it is difficult to avoid asking about its purpose. Does it serve some

9

pre-ordained teleological end; or is it merely a functional device for the preservation of society?

The 'principled' refusal of hard-line realists to raise such questions is likely to be defended on the grounds that the political realm is a self-contained world with its own rules of logic and discourse which do not require them to stray beyond its boundaries, indeed which positively require them to stay within them. But if it is correct to argue that some principle of order is implicit in their position, smuggled in, as it were, while they were looking in the other direction, then it may be the case that hard-line realism is an impossible position. If there was no such principle, there would surely be a total rather than a relative absence of tranquillity in the world. No doubt its denial represents a powerful psychological posture, to which many of us are prone, in much the same way as we are prone to anxiety dreams, but ultimately it is not sustainable.

On this view of the matter it is their opponents who have the better of the argument. This is because the problem for the hard-line realists is to account (within a view of the world in which ultimately conflict is the one organising principle), for such order and peace as occasionally breaks out. The soft opposition does not have to face this problem quite so early, or in quite so uncompromising a form. As we shall see, however, in the end, they may not be any better off.

They do not generally deny either the central importance of conflict in human affairs, or the primacy of the sovereign state. However, their position can be distinguished from that of their more uncompromising opponents in two ways. First, unlike hard-line realists, they accept that political obligation does not stop at the frontier, that the mutual recognition of sovereigns constitutes, or rather requires there to be, a wider international order or society of states. Secondly, having posited this requirement, they cannot evade the question of derivation. If, despite the absence of any physical correlate (such as territory provides for both the sovereign state and society), an international order or society of states can be said to exist, why is this so, on what is it grounded and of what does it consist?

THE SOURCES OF ORDER

There are, it seems to me, only three possible answers to these questions. Since I shall be primarily concerned here with the second of these answers let me briefly mention the other two – the list merely indicates their chronological sequence. The first answer derives international society from divine purpose: the world of apparently conflicting principalities and powers is to be understood ultimately in terms of a God-given, infinitely complex but ultimately harmonious design. The separate and independent states are so many experiments in human sociability, all of which are subsumed within a natural community of mankind. The third answer is that provided by the historicists, namely, that international society is a staging post in an evolutionary process through which mankind will fulfil its destiny, and the understanding of which alone can disclose to us the crucial distinction between the human and natural worlds. This thesis, in various guises, has been advanced by idealist, materialist and existentialist thinkers.

The second answer attempts to retain the appeal to natural reason but dispenses with the necessity of divine sanction. There are three variants.

Natural morality

The original variant maintains that the international order, as much as domestic society, is both a reflection and requirement of a *human nature* which is biased towards the good. Hugo Grotius, the seventeenth-century Dutch international lawyer, claimed that the law, including the law of war, the rights and obligations of sovereigns towards one another and the institutions of the society of states would continue to exist even if there was no God since it was reason which defined human nature.[6] And as reason was natural, so was morality.

Secular rationalism

The second variant is the secular rationalism that flowered during the European Enlightenment. Once it became possible to view human society in essentially mechanical terms, it was possible to dispense not only with God, but also with any *explicit* moral rationale for political organisation either within the state or between states. The new perspective also allowed the balance of power to be seen as a reflection of the same automatic harmony of interests which, at the level of individual human behaviour, was capable of translating private vice into public virtue. It is because the mechanical model of international politics builds in (and so renders invisible) its moral justification, rather like rust-proofing in a modern automobile, that I suggested earlier it represented the only conception of an international order that a hard-pressed realist might be persuaded to endorse. Only error in understanding the mechanism could corrupt the machine; and error could be avoided if states, no less than individuals, gave undivided attention to the pursuit of their own interests. Ironically, it was liberals rather than realists who developed this seductive variant of natural law, although it has certainly helped realists to come to terms with the conditions of modern interdependence between states.

Functionalism

It is a striking feature of these explanations of order that they have nothing to say about actual societies, let alone about the people who compose them. Indeed, one suspects that a large part of their con-tinuing attraction for the modern 'scientific' mind is their abstract impersonal quality: order does not spring from the efforts of particular men attempting to come to terms with the fatality of human division and the contingency of political conflict. Nor is it based on a moral vision of the good life, or at least a set of moral precepts. It springs from a general and immutable attribute of human nature. The final variant retains this preference for an abstract and general explanation, and again makes no attempt to provide a moral justification for social and political arrangements. It shifts the emphasis, from nature to nurture, or rather from the proposition that order is a reflection of a specifically human nature to the proposition that it is a functional, i.e., self-preserving, requirement of all human societies.

Those who have viewed the international problem from this func-tionalist perspective have tended to take the customs and conventions of the society of states for granted. Instead they concentrate on the deeper question of how order is possible at all in the absence of any supranational government or authority. Their quest has appeared increasingly urgent, as the major powers, driven forward by the realist logic, have developed weapons of mass destruction of increasing range and sophistication.

On one view, the problem is complicated still further by the erosion of religious faith, and by the elevation of nationalism in its place, in many of the world's most powerful societies. If, as Durkheim argued,[7] societies invent God as a means of worshipping themselves and thus bonding their individual members together in the act of Communion, what is to happen when this invention becomes widely known? The power of religion depends largely on the solution it offers to the mystery of human existence. It is this which unites the believers. But when religion is relativised, and God becomes just another national deity, whose success is ultimately to be measured by His upward mobility in a world of rivals, what then? Will the secularisation of society not inevitably open the door to unscrupulous leaders whose worldly ambitions are unconstrained by any acknowledgement of transcendental authority? These frightening questions have lain before us at least since the French Revolution.

Whatever *impasse* the logic of our arguments leads us into, human beings have invariably allowed themselves to hope. Without such a major concession to 'irrationality' it would be impossible, it seems to me, to account for creativity. We continue to need miracles; indeed, at a time when there is a real danger of the arms race being carried beyond the earth's atmosphere, we stand more in need of a miracle, of a gigantic shift in human consciousness and vision, than ever before. But creativity, the ability, by the power of imagination, to put into the world something which was not there before, or to restore to it something which has been lost, is an activity which social theorists are ill-equipped to perform. Miracles are precisely those events which cannot be explained, let alone explained away.

No wonder then that soft-liners have looked around for models of social organisation which, if they can be shown to fit, might suggest that humanity is not hell-bent on self-destruction. One promising model has seemed to many to be provided by those pre-literate stateless societies, i.e., societies which lack central institutions of government and administration but which nevertheless have mechanisms for resolving disputes and containing conflict at a level where it does not threaten the existence of the group.

The argument runs roughly as follows. If the Nuer of the southern Sudan have survived without the assistance of a state, perhaps international society, which is also characterised by an absence of government, may be structured in a similar way. After all, it also has its diplomatic rituals and conventional ways of carrying on business even during a violent conflict – think for example of the role of neutrals. Pastoral societies, arguably, provide the best analogue for the international order because of their high level of dependence on armaments at the individual and clan level, just as at state and alliance level in international society. Pastoral societies, like modern states in their relations with one another, are fiercely egalitarian, which prevents them from accepting for long any settled system of central authority. They are also fiercely competitive, which leads them into loose alliances and all manner of subterfuges, the point of which is to acquire not parity or equilibrium but supremacy, to amass more cattle, sheep, goats or camels than their opponents.

There is a saving grace to this forbidding prospect: pastoralists appear to know that if the game is to continue – and it is to this game

13

that their way of life commits them – they must not press their rivalries to the point of destroying the grazing, the one resource on which they all depend. In an essay, written in 1959, in which he surveyed the nuclear prospect, Ernest Gellner allowed himself hope that the human habitat might be saved by some analogous hidden mechanism, not the cunning of reason or of history favoured by historicist thinkers, but the cunning, so to speak, of species preservation.[8] In a similar vein, the late Raymond Aron argued consistently that at least so far mankind had saved itself by allowing for the possibility of war.[9]

Such conjectures allow soft-liners to hope, against the contradictory evidence of contemporary international life, that there may after all be a moral justification for our current arrangements. The contradictions in the evidence are indeed spectacular: if there is no practical option but to pursue our political objectives within a 'real', limited, more or less culturally specific social context (whatever the position may theoretically have been, within medieval Christendom or Umma Islam), how are we possibly to limit the conflicts of interest and passion which, now as in the past, are inherent in any system in which there is more than one centre of political power and authority?

In the final analysis, functionalism fails to provide a satisfactory answer to this question. The whole aim of the functionalist endeavour is to uncover hidden mechanisms of order, which are built-in and so pattern human behaviour irrespective of our self-consciously held values, the narcissistic policies of governments, or our deliberate intentions for good or ill. But even to write this sentence is to point to its central weakness: there can be no such endeavour unless we accept in advance the possibility and point of self-conscious reflection and analysis. And if we allow ourselves cognitive freedom in this way, must we not also concede that intentions and motives have a direct bearing on outcomes in the world of action.

There are dangers in building a model of international society on this, as on any other form of domestic analogy. However deep their feuds, pastoralists will typically share much more than their common grazing, for example, a language, a religion or even a common ancestor, any one of which can be invoked in the interests of conflict resolution. The member states of international society, by contrast, are culturally diverse and seldom – despite the fashionable and optimistic talk about the global commons – share resources let alone fundamental beliefs at all.[10] Indeed, it is not clear that modern international society constitutes a form of life, as pastoralism, or hunting and gathering or industrialism can be said to do. And if it does not,

14

we cannot confidently predict that certain safety mechanisms are built-in to the international condition.

Despite the idea of rational irrationality on which the idea of nuclear deterrence is ultimately based, we can have no final confidence in its efficacy. We must hope that it will work but there is no reason to be sanguine. Already the history of the twentieth century, the century *par excellence* of scientific rationality and constant technological advance, is replete with horror stories. Political crimes have been carried out on a scale and with a self-conscious deliberation and ferocity which is unprecedented. They have been perpetuated, in the name of historical necessity, progress, the destiny of a particular master race, or for no clearly stated reason at all. Against such a background how can we be sure that the powers will never again pursue their conflicts of interest, ideological rivalries and mass hatreds to the point of cultural genocide and/or mutual suicide? We cannot.

I suggested earlier that in the implicit debate within western state theory, those who qualify the rigours of undiluted power politics by acknowledging that the states participate in a wider system have the better of the argument. For the hard-line realist the only possible international order is a contingent by-product of the state's single-minded pursuit of its self-interest. Soft-liners at least accept the maintenance of order amongst their objectives. But having reviewed the various positions which are available for grounding this order, one can only conclude that while their position remains more sympathetic than that of the hard-line realists, and while intuitively it seems to accord with at least some aspects of our experience of contemporary international life, it still begs more questions than it answers.

A RETREAT TO DESCRIPTION

To repeat the central questions: is there, or is there not, an international system or society which can provide us with that minimal security which the state is said to have a duty to provide within its own borders? If there is such a system what is the mechanism or means by which it discharges the functions which, within the state, are discharged by the government? And if such mechanisms or means can in turn be said to exist, what is their status and on what are they grounded? Many contemporary observers argue backwards from the alleged existence of the safety mechanism – the system of deterrence – to a body of shared understandings.[11] Concealed under layers of ideological disputation, they detect common

15

interests and values, above all the interest of survival, which together may be said to constitute the international order or society.

We have seen that the ground on which functional mechanisms rest, and deterrence is surely one of these, is anything but solid. Arguments can certainly be advanced for believing in the mechanism. For example, in all pre-nuclear wars, however terrible, it has been possible to conceive politically of the spoils of victory. Such a conception makes no sense in the case of a nuclear exchange. But there are equally powerful arguments on the other side. For example, historically, balances of power have always proved unstable over the long run, while, in the end, arms races have always led to war. Even if, on optimistic assumptions, the system of deterrence can be viewed as an institution of order, it is difficult to view the nuclear arms race in the same light.

Realists who attempt to soften their vision by supporting it with a functionalist account of order are, in effect, treating an optimistic, although reasonable conjecture, as though it was an explanation. And as with any conjecture, there is not much more to be said; less indeed than with most conjectures where one can at least calculate the odds on the basis of past experience. In the case of a nuclear war, it either will happen or it will not. If deterrence continues to operate we may conclude that there are limits to the anarchy of international life; if it fails the question will be of no further interest anyway.

If, as has so far been implied, there is no unambiguously satisfactory explanation of international order, it is perhaps not surprising that most students of the subject content themselves with describing what, from such evidence as they have available to them, appears to have happened. One such account is that which describes the society of states, and the principles of order on which it is based, as having developed out of the breakdown of the 'universal' world of medieval Christendom, and in its final codified form, out of the peace settlement which ended the Thirty Years War. One advantage of this account is that it provides a picture of international society before the age of nationalism, and therefore also a measure against which to assess its impact.

It will no doubt be objected that this retreat to description is a subterfuge, that an explanatory model, and the values on which it is based, has been smuggled in under the guise of an objective neutrality. I do not wish to deny it, or to suggest that as a solution to the problem of international order it is satisfactory – indeed in large part the point of the preceding discussion has been to demonstrate its vulnerability. But I do maintain that this conventional account of the international society, the principles of which were codified at West-phalia in 1648, is the one against which most nationalists first formula-ted their rival vision of the world, and which those of them who were successful subsequently adapted to their own purposes. It is, there-fore, to the Westphalian system, first in its original form and then under the impact of nationalism that we must now turn.

2 THE SOCIETY OF STATES

The design of the society of states is extremely simple. The model is derived from the principles on which the seventeenth-century European peace treaties were based and from the assumptions, requirements and additions which were introduced by the conference diplomacy of the eighteenth and nineteenth centuries.[1] The model rests firstly on an agreed legal settlement, and secondly, and more contentiously, on an institutionalised political dispensation.

THE TRADITIONAL MODEL

The legal settlement is based on the repudiation of the principle of hierarchy in inter-state relations, and consequently on an affirmation of the principle of the sovereign equality of states. The political dispensation, by contrast, involved the major powers in acknowledging to each other that, not withstanding the legal equality of all states, they had special responsibilities for maintaining international order; and consequently, that this gave them the right, if necessary, to override general international law.[2] In other words, while questions of status and right are distinguished from those of power and military capability, the separation is not total. In ways which have always seemed as suspect to the weak as they have seemed obvious to the strong, the legal order has been subordinated, not all the time, but at critical points, to the will of the powerful. While small states frequently complained about their treatment at the hands of the major powers, in the end, they could do little to change their role as consumers of whatever 'order' was created by the great powers of the day. On occasions, such as when one of them had its neutrality guaranteed, they might even benefit from it. Let us look in more detail at these two dimensions in turn.

The legal settlement

By basing the system on the principle of sovereignty, the Westphalian settlement guaranteed that so long as it persisted there could be no escape from its fundamental paradox. This paradox stems from the nature of sovereignty itself. The principle of sovereignty claims that there is a single source of authority within the state and none beyond it; hence, if sovereigns are to conclude an agreement it can only be from the standpoint of their equality, regardless of the fact that in its substantive provisions, the agreement may reflect an unequal distribution of power between the parties.

There are four entailments of any settlement based on the principle of sovereignty. First, if sovereign authorities are to conclude agreements, they must recognise one another as sovereign. Since no authority higher than the state exists, without recognition there would be no possibility of securing a legal settlement of the inter-state problem at all. Secondly, it follows from the nature of the settlement between authorities whose claim to a monopoly of jurisdiction within the state is recognised by their peers, that any agreement between them will have to be either self-policing, or it will have to rely on policing by the separate parties themselves. The former would require the settlement to be so securely based on the reciprocated self-interest of the parties that there would be no incentive to break it; the latter the knowledge that a failure to enforce the agreement would risk reprisals if not its total breakdown.

This latter possibility is the only one available if the idea of lawful behaviour is to be extended to the conduct of warfare, that aspect of human conduct which most notoriously calls in question the reality of any over-arching 'system', or at the very least reveals the fundamental paradox of this system in its most acute form. It does so because, by its nature, any agreement which is policed by the parties themselves is one which is open to abuse; there being nothing to prevent them acting as judge and jury in their own cause.

The conceptual difficulties involved were vividly illustrated at the Nuremberg and Tokyo trials after the Second World War.[3] Because of the peculiarly awful nature of the Nazi regime in particular, the attempt to move beyond the traditional concept of a victor's peace to the concept of justiciable war crimes and crimes against humanity was widely felt to represent not only a legitimate development of international law but a strong assertion of commonly held international values. But the legality of this extension of traditional practice has frequently been challenged and has not since been applied in any other international conflict.

The third entailment of a system based on the principle of sovereignty is the translation of territory from being just somewhere where people hunt, or farm or go to the factory into the ultimate object of political life. A crucial distinction between traditional forms of society (for example feudalism) and modern society is the distinction between a world in which what mattered was having power over people and one in which what matters is having power over things. A system based on the acceptance of many different sovereign authorities, is a system based on the sanctity of property. The inter-state system, depicted in the conventional model, is a real estate model: the value which sovereign states can not sacrifice without, as it were, committing suicide, is their independence. What this means in practice is that they cannot surrender their territorial integrity.

The final, most important but also most problematic entailment of the principle of sovereignty is the requirement of non-interference in the domestic affairs of other states. It is the most important entailment because it provides the basic element of trust, without which sovereign authorities would be most unlikely to enter into agreements at all. They have always been neurotically although understandably jealous of their claims to supremacy. If powers which are not subject to the jurisdiction of the state are to be *permitted* to dictate the course of its political life, what is left of the concept of sovereignty? In such circumstances it would no longer be merely paradoxical, it would become radically incoherent.

Non-interference is the most problematic entailment of sovereignty, however, because, by asserting an absolute prohibition, it appears to make an immoral principle a crucial structural support of the system. It is as well to be clear on this point. The principle of non-interference in domestic affairs is *not* an edict of toleration except in a highly restricted context. The original formula – *cuius regio eius religio* – from which the modern version is derived, was no doubt essential, certainly useful, in calling a halt to a morally debilitating and materially destructive ideological war. But as in all compromises there was a price to be paid. That price was to sanction any amount of religious intolerance – and Luther and Calvin embraced the principle of intolerance with just as much enthusiasm as did the Inquisition – within the sovereign territory of the Prince.

Modern attempts to breach the non-interference principle in the interests of protecting fundamental human rights (and I am referring here to the theoretical and legal debate on this issue rather than to state practice) invariably, and inevitably, run up against the core doctrine of sovereignty.

Sovereigns, whether they are dynasts, tyrants, or democratically elected governments, may subscribe publicly to the view that their own rule is dependent on their protection of such rights, but they *never* surrender their sole authority to interpret the definition and meaning of human rights within their own jurisdiction. The rights in question are said to be human, to derive not from an act of specific historical creation, but to inhere in our humanity. However, where they are honoured, as in the European Convention, which Sieghart rightly regards as 'a substantial retreat from the previously sacred principle of national sovereignty', it is, *in fact*, because of the conventional, reciprocal agreement between sovereigns not because of their ahistorical self-evidence.[4]

To rebut this argument, it would be necessary to claim that rights could exist independently of a consciousness of their existence, that, for example, participation in the feudal compact, with its hierarchical conception of rights and obligations, was not only historically doomed but without moral justification even in its heyday. How, without recourse to a higher authority, can such a claim possibly be supported? The question is, of course, rhetorical. It may be objected that it conflates (and confuses) two questions, one about the logical coherence of human rights theories, the other about the historical contexts in which they were advanced. But if, as suggested here, it is possible to envisage such theories being advanced in some kinds of society, but not in others, it is difficult to avoid the conclusion that there is a symbiotic relationship between them.

If, therefore, as moral beings we are led to accept that some ordering principle is necessary in relations between independent political communities, we are also led in the direction of challenging the basis of the only conceivable ordering principle that we can come up with, namely political consensus. We can intuitively sympathise with those who forged the idea of a system based on non-interference – in human terms it was indeed an immense achievement – but if it is advanced as an absolute, it inevitably offends our moral sensibility. There must surely be *some* circumstances when it is right to ignore the prohibition? If this is so, we have no alternative but to choose when to uphold, and when to breach, the principle. And the reality, but also the agony of such a choice, is that we have no solid ground on which to base a decision to override the non-interference principle. In the one case – agreement on non-interference – intuition is based on experience: all agreements require compromise, something has to be given up. In the other case – choosing to breach the principle – intuition is based on itself: there is no sure basis for action, no external, reciprocated, agreement that what is an outrage, is, *in fact*, an outrage. This is the inescapable moral problem which arises, within the conventional model, from its legal settlement. It is not obvious that a solution exists; but it is undeniably a problem.

21

The political dispensation

If the legal structure of the society of states is radically egalitarian, its political structure remains stubbornly hierarchical. In any political system there has to be an accommodation between power and law, that is, between the relations of force and those of right; indeed the fact that there is such an accommodation is what enables us to identify a political system and to distinguish it from other forms of human association, for example a family or a mob. Within most modern political systems the legal requirement of equality is generally reconciled with the uneven distribution of natural and acquired capabilities by investing the state with a monopoly of *legitimate* force. Because there is no world state, it is at this point that the domestic analogy breaks down as a way of describing the inter-state system. For the same reason there is also an unusual and striking mis-match between the egalitarian order of law and the hierarchical order of power in international politics.

In the absence of other comparative material, there is no alternative but to persist with the domestic analogy, albeit forewarned of its inadequacy, in order to identify the peculiar relationship between law and power which characterises the inter-state system. If, as I have just argued, adherence to the non-interference principle may lead to an inescapable moral dilemma, namely how to reconcile support for the order which is built on the principle's absolute pretensions, with the discretionary right to take action in defiance of the principle under exceptional circumstances, this dilemma is essentially the same for great and small powers alike. Compare, for example, the Tanzanian intervention in Uganda in 1979, and the American intervention in Grenada in 1984. There were certain similarities: the Tanzanian government was determined to unseat the Ugandan dictator, Idi Amin, and the American government to restore a democratic government in Grenada after its head of state and a number of his political colleagues had been murdered in a conspiratorial uprising.

Depending on our point of view we may judge the merits of these two interventions differently, ascribing more or less weight to considerations of self-interest, political calculation and expediency in each case. The consequences for the Tanzanian economy and society were undoubtedly far more extensive than for the United States. Nonetheless it is clear that the underlying nature of the choice to ignore the terms of the legal settlement was essentially the same in both cases. It is tempting to conclude, therefore, that states which decide, for whatever reason, to breach the non-interference principle, are in the same case as citizens who, for whatever reason, decide to break the law. But is this so?

Within a democratic constitution, the central function of the law is to ensure that power and wealth are neutralised in disputes between citizens. Indeed, it is precisely the weak and underprivileged who stand most in need of an impartial legal order. No doubt there is no country where theory and practice exactly coincide, where privilege can never be purchased and corruption of public officials never occurs. But very few of those who argue that the law is always designed merely to protect the existing power structure within the state would, I imagine, choose to live in a lawless state where there was no hypocrisy, no ambiguity and no way of arguing with naked force.

It is true that, within the state, any citizen may have to face a crisis of conscience as a result of which he or she has to choose whether or not to obey a particular law. At first sight this indeed seems analogous to the dilemma which a sovereign government may have to face if it decides to breach the non-interference principle. But the analogy is not exact. Within the state, force is monopolised in order that private power should not decide the outcome of civil disputes; a private citizen who disobeys the law on a question of conscience may hope to change it through an appeal to public opinion, but if she or he is not successful, then that is the end of the matter. A state which decides to ignore the non-interference principle is deliberately putting the issue to the test of force; it may or may not succeed in its objective, but it certainly intends to try.

The relations between law and force in international politics are thus not the same as those found in other political systems. To understand the political dispensation in the traditional model, therefore, we must return to the original peace treaty on which it was based. What was established at Westphalia was not remotely like a liberal constitutional state; nor was it like an absolutist state. The sovereigns agreed that religious differences should no longer constitute a legitimate *causus belli*; they did not renounce the use of force. On the contrary, by declaring an ideological ceasefire, they left themselves free to go to war for any reason of state that might present itself. In these circumstances while they called a halt to a particular war, they effectively turned inter-state rivalry, preparation for war and ultimately war itself into an institution of the system along with diplomacy and the law of coexistence.

How, within such a system, can there be any order, any relief from the constant manoeuvring and battling of the powers? The conventional answer to this question is that there can be no relief from the

23

manoeuvring which is inherent in any system which is built on rivalry, for the reasons accurately diagnosed by Thomas Hobbes in the passage quoted in the previous chapter. But it does not follow from this that the war will be perpetual and totally destructive of all order in international relations. Once ideological warfare has been ruled out by the agreement of the powers, force will be used as a political instrument to achieve limited political ends, not to bring about the total destruction of the enemy state or the elimination of its political identity; at least this is how it will be used in theory. Self-interest will thus ensure that force is not used unless there is a reasonable expectation of success, and since there is no appeal from a defeat in battle, that it will only be used as a last resort.

The system we are discussing developed from a peace settlement. The signatories had been involved, in one way or another, in the war which preceded it. The boundaries of the system were thus, in an important sense, the boundaries of the battlefield, the area in which, momentarily at least, the guns had been silenced. Under the terms of the settlement, the titanic ideological struggle between the forces of good and evil, truth and error, which had allowed the war to engulf the whole continent (and in the process had allowed many old scores to be settled, and provided scope for the pursuit of numerous more mundane ambitions), was finally ended. By the same token this gave to those great powers, whose rivalries and capabilities were on a scale that could again threaten general war, a decisive voice in shaping the new order. What came to be known as the balance of power between these major powers gradually emerged in the eighteenth century as the central ordering mechanism of the system.

Judged by the frequency with which it broke down, the institution of a balance or equilibrium between the great powers was, when compared with the institution of government within the state, a very poor substitute for the legal monopoly of force. But, so the conventional argument runs, given the independence of states it was the only substitute there was.[5] Be that as it may – and it must be admitted that the stillborn alternatives envisaged in the collective security arrangements of the League of Nations and the United Nations Security Council provide strong supporting evidence – the fact that the military balance between the major powers acts as the basic political principle of the system, just as sovereignty acts as its basic legal principle, exposes a further paradoxical feature of the entire design.

It is the legal settlement which opens up possibilities of peaceful diplomacy, commerce and the regulated movement of people across political frontiers. By so doing, it also allows us to talk of an inter-state system. Yet, in the final analysis, this legal settlement is subordinated to the requirements of the balance of power. As a result, those who can influence the balance can, and always have, justified their actions, when these contradict the legal settlement, by reference to the priority which must be accorded to international order on which the whole edifice is held to rest. Thus was Poland partitioned at the end of the eighteenth century to preserve the balance of power amongst the European powers and Africa divided in 1884 to prevent the scramble for colonies precipitating a more dangerous European conflict.

It is hardly surprising that this aspect of the system has never been popular with the smaller powers. In the pre-nationalist era their criticism was masked, or at least muted, by the values and assumptions about political life which were widely shared by the ruling class throughout Europe. From a sociological and cultural perspective, the European inter-state system was relatively homogenous. The rise of nationalism shattered this homogenised world of shared values and assumptions, and led the small powers, and those disenfranchised nations which sought to become powers, to denounce the paradox as a contradiction. It is time, therefore, to ask how the traditional model has stood up under this new challenge?

THE IMPACT OF NATIONALISM

The answer to this question is deeply ambiguous. Since the French Revolution the assumptions, practices and institutions of the traditional world have been repeatedly challenged by nationalist forces in different parts of the world. At one level of analysis this challenge has been enormously successful. The ultimate measure of that success is the difficulty that people have everywhere (perhaps particularly in the west where the challenge was first mounted), in envisaging an alternative political form to that of the nation-state.[6] In the modern world the relations of governments, as much as those of peoples, are invariably described as inter*national* relations; to describe them in any other way would be pedantic. Except to a handful of scholars, nationalism is not a problem; rather national sentiment is so pervasive and self-evident that it has become invisible. The pathological excesses of nationalism which have exacted such an horrendous price in human lives in the twentieth century do, of course, attract much wider attention, but they are invariably diagnosed in terms of their own symptoms, not in terms of the healthy, i.e., 'natural' organism.

At another level, however, the traditional model proved much stronger than the forces arrayed against it. The nationalists, it is true, moved into the building which had previously been occupied by dynastic rulers and religious authorities, creating in the process much new real estate. However, the new sub-divisions, like so many condominiums and flying freeholds, left the building itself more or less intact. In other words, they were more often forced to accommodate their own plans to the existing structure, than they were able to rebuild the international system in their own image. And when they did succeed in bringing about a modification, it was seldom an unequivocal moral improvement. The world of power politics remains intact; indeed arguably the major impact of nationalism has been to reinforce the tradition of hard-line realism, and to weaken the version in which the inerradicable egotism of the separate state was at least softened by a residual solidarity amongst states.

The remainder of this book will discuss this process of challenge and accommodation in more detail. Before embarking on this discussion, it will be useful to review the conventional model in the light of the three major modifications which are closely linked with it, even if they do not always result directly from the nationalist challenge. These modifications are concerned with the principle of political legitimacy on which the system is built, the role of force within it and most obviously with its universalisation.

International legitimacy

It is, it seems to me, a mistake to draw a distinction between domestic principles of political legitimacy and those that obtain in international relations. The legal settlement in the traditional system was based on the principle of sovereignty. The question of the grounding of sovereignty itself was not addressed; indeed it was a necessary condition of the new order that it should not be addressed, since within Christendom it was no longer in order to dispute the mandate of heaven. But, in fact, the settlement was between sovereign kings and princes, hereditary monarchs who, within their own realms and principalities, were anxious to bolster their prescriptive right to rule with whatever metaphysical supports were ready to hand.

It is true that in the dramatic, as much as the political literature of the seventeenth century, in Calderón and in Shakespeare as well as in Hobbes, the great debate about the nature of kingship and its relationship to common humanity is already prefigured. A potentially relativist chink had been opened in their defences which would eventually lead to the overthrow of the dynasts. The king of Poland, in Calderón's *Life is a Dream* tries to find out whether inborn nobility or sombre predictions of astrology will govern the behaviour of his son once he is released from the dungeon where he has been thrown at birth. Lear needs his fool to build him up as well as to cut him down to size. But if the question was everywhere being raised in the seventeenth century, nowhere was it being answered. For the moment the underlying principle of legitimacy, in the inter-state system, as well as at home, remained dynastic. Rulers might choose for prudential or other reasons to mobilise popular, even national, sentiment on their own behalf, as Queen Elizabeth of England did so effectively at Tilbury, but they did not have to. The world was a world of subjects not of citizens.

From the time of the great revolutions onwards, the dynastic principle came under sustained and increasingly successful attack. A new principle of international legitimacy, which again mirrored the domestic arrangements of the major powers, was advanced and eventually gained, at least a theoretical ascendency over the system as a whole. This was the principle of popular sovereignty. Its elevation was intimately related to the rise of nationalist sentiment and the political demands of nationalist doctrine, first in Europe and then further afield. The case for the new principle was eloquently expounded by John Stuart Mill in 1861:

> Where the sentiment of nationality exists in any force, there is a *prima facie* case for uniting all the members of the nationality under the same government, and a government to themselves apart. This is merely saying that the question of government ought to be decided by the governed. One hardly knows what any division of the human race should be free to do if not to determine with which of the various collective bodies of human beings they choose to associate themselves.[7]

When Mill wrote *Representative Government* the new principle of political legitimacy was still being actively contested. But in the century that followed his arguments swept the board. Indeed the argument for self-government was reinforced by another which is implicit in Mill's account, namely that national self-determination is a necessary, if not sufficient condition of international peace and security. Thus Article 1(ii) of the United Nations Charter calls on the member states 'to develop friendly relations among nations based on respect for the principle of equal rights and self-determination of peoples, and to take appropriate measures to strengthen universal peace'. This formula is repeated in Article 55 which sets out the goal of social and economic cooperation and respect for fundamental human rights and was strengthened still further in 1960 – by the passage of

General Assembly Resolution 1514 which ruled that lack of preparation for self-rule should not be accepted as a legitimate reason for delaying independence. Finally, Article 1 of the two United Nations Conventions of Civil and Political Rights, and of Economic, Social and Cultural Rights, agreed in 1966, assert that 'all peoples have the right of self-determination'.

There is one qualification which should be entered to the proposition that the principle of international legitimacy in the contemporary system, as in the traditional model, mirrors the prevailing principle of political legitimacy within the state. It is this. In the traditional world despite the cautious epistemological probing of the poets and the philosophers (was a king naturally royal or just a man with the ambition or good fortune to find himself in a position of power?) political scepticism was not profound. The princes who met at Westphalia were all princes and they recognised each other as such. Since the people were not involved in the settlement, there was less need for hypocrisy, the price that vice so regularly pays to virtue, than in the model modified under the impact of nationalism.

This qualification is important because hypocrisy is unavoidable in any discussion of the principle of international legitimacy in the modern world, while there is room for debate about the role that it plays in discussions of the basis of popular sovereignty in different countries. The formal order is still defined by the mutual recognition of sovereign states; but sovereignty is now said to reside with the people, as the result of an act of national self-determination based on the will of the majority. Since this is not an accurate description of the position in very many contemporary states, including many of those whose governments champion the principle most loudly, it is not surprising that those who are most often singled out for criticism on the grounds that they offend against the new principle of legitimacy, for example, South Africa and Israel, accuse their critics of hypocrisy and deny that the modified legal settlement bears any relationship to reality. They are right on the first count – their critics frequently *are* hypocritical – but wrong on the second. All that has happened is that the system has become culturally and politically more heterogeneous with the result that the gap between the formal order of international society, and what, in fact, goes on in particular societies, has widened.

The legitimate use of force

Under the *ancien régime* war was accepted almost as part of the natural order; it might be regrettable but so were other natural disasters which were periodically inflicted on suffering humanity such as famine or plague. There was little to be done about it not least because those states with the capability to influence the balance of power regarded war not only as a legitimate instrument of policy but as an institution of the system. What was the impact of nationalism on this aspect of the traditional order?

The answer to this question is complex. It is difficult to avoid the conclusion that it has made matters worse, that is, that nationalism has contributed to the increasing destructiveness of modern wars and the progressive militarisation of the planet. This possibility was vaguely sensed in the liberal attack on the *ancien régime* but was generally discounted on the grounds that national self-determination was a necessary precondition for the evolution of a rational social order. Thus Mill wrote:

> If it be said that so broadly marked distinction [i.e. nationality] between what is due to a fellow countryman and what is due merely to a human creature is more worthy of savages than of civilised beings, and ought with the utmost energy to be contended against, no one holds that opinion more strongly than myself. But this object, one of the worthiest to which human endeavour can be directed, can never, in the present state of civilisation, be promoted by keeping different nationalities of anything like equivalent strength under the same government.[8]

Opponents of any system tend not to see its merits so long as they are intent on its overthrow. The traditional inter-state system had produced an environment which favoured two developments, neither of which at first sight seemed likely to appeal to the nationalist temperament. The first related to the role of force within the legal settlement, the second to its use in support of the political dispensation; together they effectively constituted a war compact.

The legal settlement made possible the elaboration of the laws of war, the deliberate attempt to mark war off from random violence by distinguishing between belligerents and civilians, and the behaviour appropriate in each case, to define legitimate and illegitimate weaponry, to prescribe the proper treatment of prisoners of war, and so on. Indeed arguably the major achievement of the advocates of international society, whose position I sketched in the previous chapter, was to 'civilise' war by shifting the emphasis on *ius ad bellum*, the concept of a just war, to *ius in bello*, the concept of a fair fight.[9]

The second development was the growth of military science. Once war was established as a legal institution of the system, it was possible to construct 'rational' theories, the basic point of which was to

29

illuminate the way in which force could be deliberately and self-consciously used to achieve limited political objectives. Clausewitz, above all, saw the necessity of this development if violent conflict, fuelled by passion and knowing no natural restraint, was to be subordinated to political control and calculation.[10]

It is with these permissive but cold, calculating and legalistic attitudes towards war that nationalists have to contend. When one recalls that nationalist doctrine requires that the political map be redrawn according to the principle of sentimental attachment and identity, it is not surprising that nationalists found the war compact uncongenial. At the same time, the nature of the modifications in this aspect of the traditional model which the nationalists have wrought, is itself contested.

The contest arises because there are two major strands of nationalist thought, liberal and historicist, which have affected not only the interpretation of international politics but its organisation. At the level of the formal order it was the liberal nationalists who inherited the mantle of Grotian orthodoxy: national self-determination was, and remains, as we shall see in the next chapter, a liberal principle and the liberals share with Grotians a conception of solidarity beyond that of the nation-state. But liberal thinkers were, generally speaking, optimists and men of peace. Above all they objected to the idea that the cause of freedom and self-determination could be served by the deliberate use of force except in the limiting case of resistance to oppression or direct attack. They sought, therefore, not to banish force from the world, that was beyond their immediate abilities although not beyond their dreams, but to limit its use to self-defence. The line stretches from Kant's essay on *Perpetual Peace* published in 1795,[11] through Woodrow Wilson's project for collective security in the League of Nations Covenant, to the more 'realistic' version contained in the United Nations Charter. In the modified version of international society, which the liberal nationalists envisaged, war was not a rational policy instrument, let alone an institution or mechanism for maintaining the balance of power; it was a breakdown of international order, an atavistic and uncontrollable retreat into the irrational world.

The formal triumph of liberal thought on the use of force for political ends has been spectacular. Not only has conquest been ruled out as a means of acquiring prescriptive rights over either territory or people, but no government (with the possible exception of the Chinese), will openly advance its forces against those of another country unless it can claim that it has been attacked, has been forced to act in order to pre-empt an attack, or has been invited into a country in order to

30

restore order. But this triumph is weakened not merely by the fact that self-defence is a malleable concept, notoriously open to abuse by political interests, but because, as an allegedly logical system of ideas, liberalism has no developed theory of historical change. For many liberals the idea of progress is an integral part of their world view and political beliefs. But since, for them, progress manifests itself through the rational (read peaceful) development of society, they have no consistent way of accounting for the role of force in the founding of legitimate national states.

Precisely because they have no theory of historical development, liberals tend to be armchair nationalists. They are able to grasp intellectually that a community may be bound together by common memories, above all of common suffering. But they seldom feel the emotional force of the nationalist position, namely that a national community is one which shares a common view of itself located in history, with particular origins and a common destiny. These are not optional extras but the definition of an existential reality.

Not surprisingly, historicist nationalists take a different view of the legitimate role of force in international politics than their liberal counterparts. In their case, it seems to me, the line can be traced from Hegel's insistence that the conquests of the historical nations contribute to human progress,[12] through the frenzied enthusiasm of the belligerents during the early stages of the First World War, all of whom believed in their historical destiny, to the contemporary scene of freedom fighters engaged in real and imaginary wars of national liberation. Because of the critical role which hindsight plays in the historicist view of the world, providing an escape clause from which there is no appeal, there is plenty of room for disputing which wars were of world historical significance, and therefore, in the final analysis morally justifiable. What is clear, is that for historicists, war is not a question of political calculation, nor can it necessarily be confined to self-defence: it is an ethical act involving a total commitment by the people to a freedom which can only be realised in a struggle with its opposite.

The major wars of the twentieth century required the mobilisation of nations, their civilian populations, economic resources and productive effort, as well as their uniformed military guardians. A nation in arms fights not for narrow political advantage but for its own survival and the survival of the civilisation it represents. In part, therefore, the nationalist modification to the traditional model – and on this score there is no great difference in the liberal and historicist versions – is to de-institutionalise war and so set the stage for a return to absolute

31

conflict. Total wars (and this applies equally to irregular guerrilla wars as to modern conventional wars) are either unjustifiable or they require a total justification.

The point of dispute between liberal and historicist nationalists occurs over the definition of an act of self-defence. By confining formal membership of international society to sovereign states, official opinion in the western democracies has generally refused to widen the concept to include armed struggle by groups within states who wish to challenge the authority and representative character of the govern-ment.[13] No doubt because at the time the major liberal democracies still possessed large overseas empires, they have always refused to accept Krishna Menon's famous definition of colonialism as a per-manent aggression, i.e., a form of structural violence.[14] On the other hand, with few exceptions, whenever nationalist movements have been successful in persuading the colonial power to negotiate by force of arms, liberal governments have recognised the successor govern-ment and so, implicitly, if after the event, accepted the legitimacy of the nationalist justification. Thus President de Gaulle, who was more willing to adopt historicist arguments in public than most western leaders, initiated his Algerian policy by offering the Front de Liber-ation National (FLN) 'a peace of the brave', the implication being that the Algerian nation had earned the right to exist by its willingness to make the ultimate sacrifice in battle.[15] Thus, too, the western demo-cracies, whose leaders made no such statements about the African Independence Party of Guinea and Cape Verde (PAIGC), or the Front for the Liberation of Mozambique (FRELIMO), let alone the Popular Movement for the Liberation of Angola (MPLA), quickly accepted the independent statehood of Guinea-Bissau, Mozambique and Angola after the collapse of the Portuguese empire in 1974.

The extension of the system

It may be argued that it is the relentless advance of technology rather than the rise of nationalist ideology that undermined the polite ethical distinctions which were possible within the traditional world. Long before the advent of nuclear weapons, so the argument runs, the invention of the submarine and the aeroplane had destroyed forever the possibility of discriminating in warfare between legitimate and illegitimate targets. In similar fashion it may be held that it was not the subversive idea of individual and collective freedom that, from small beginnings in the west, radiated outwards, thus making it possible to conceive of, and even partially achieve, a single integrated world system, it was the logic of industrial society and of the world market which this logic created.

It is not possible to settle the long-standing debate on this issue between materialists and idealists. For if we are led, following Kant, to the view that our understanding of reality is necessarily constructed by our concepts, in other words that we invent reality, we have to ask why these concepts and not others? We must also ask how is it that the concepts we have available to interpret reality do not remain constant over time? Why, for example, was the *naturalness* of hierarchy, the essential underpinning of the dynastic world, replaced by the *naturalness* of equality, the essential underpinning of the nationalist world? And is it not at least plausible that what we are able to think at any given time, using the stock of available concepts, is deeply influenced by the material circumstances in which we find ourselves? The idea of saturation bombing is unthinkable without the concept of collective responsibility, but it is also unthinkable before the invention of bombers. The idea of a world market is unthinkable without the concept of a division of labour, but also without the means of transporting goods over long distances, preserving perishable commodities over time and a convertible medium of exchange.

What we have here, it seems, is a conflict about how to describe the modifications introduced into the traditional model under the impact of nationalism. This conflict arises because of an inability to *explain* reality unambiguously. Yet, if we are to try to understand the world we have no alternative but to describe it. What then is to be done? The only way in which the descriptive strategy can be salvaged is to accept, regardless of the aesthetic cost, that the nationalist ideal and the pressures of technological progress and industrial production have constantly reinforced one another. This combination both undermined the moral coherence of the old world and helped to integrate the new world, albeit on the basis of a much less secure moral platform.

Two contrasts between the traditional model and its nationalist successor are immediately apparent. The first is that the boundaries of the inter-state system have been pushed out to a point where they are coextensive with those of the globe. This is the result of the irresistible appeal of the doctrine of national self-determination and the equally undeniable fact that a general war would now engulf the world.

The second observation is that this horizontal extension of traditional international society has been complemented by a vertical extension through the penetration of central government activity downwards into the lives of the people and upwards into the regulation of an ever-widening range of transnational relationships.

This second extension, like the first, has been brought about by two developments. On the one hand, it is the result of the claim that each nation has its own national economy, an inalienable patrimony, and that governments have responsibility for the welfare as well as for the physical security of their citizens. On the other it is a response to the pressures generated by coexistence within a complex division of labour. Within a multi-state but technologically integrated world there is much to be regulated; so much, perhaps too much, is regulated.

These issues are discussed in chapters 5 and 6. The horizontal extension of the international society preceded the vertical extension, so it is to the impact of nationalism on the geographical boundaries of the system, that is, to its role in the creation of new states, that we turn next.

3 NATIONALISM AND THE CREATION OF STATES

The previous chapter contained two sketches, the first of the traditional society of states, the second of the same society as modified under the impact of nationalism. These sketches focused deliberately on the essential features of the design. The hope was that this process of simplification and reduction would expose those elements in the landscape such as sovereign statehood, diplomacy, inter-state rivalry and war which have withstood the onslaught of nationalism, from those, such as the principle of dynastic legitimacy, imperial agrandisement, and political justifications for the use of force which have succumbed to it. Little was said, however, about the process by which the old model was transformed into the new. This is the purpose of the present chapter.

Essentially, my argument is that an accommodation was reached between the prescriptive principle of sovereignty and the popular principle of national self-determination. The result of this accommodation was the creation of over 100 new states and the development of the first truly global international society that the world had known. But the old world did not surrender unconditionally to the new: as in any accommodation, compromise was involved. The principle of national self-determination which was built into the new system turned out to be much less permissive, or popular, than attention to its philosophical origins and meaning might lead one to expect. Moreover, the global integration of international society on the basis of a principle of popular sovereignty was accompanied by an unprecedented attempt to *freeze* the political map.

DOCTRINE

How was this paradoxical compromise brought about? To answer this question we will need to look at the historic fate of two doctrines we have already encountered, those of sovereignty and national self-determination, out of whose ideological confrontation the contemporary order was forged. In order to understand the particular accommodation that was reached between them it will be helpful first to consider certain further aspects of the two doctrines, particularly those which lent themselves to compromise.

Sovereignty

Removed from the historical context in which the doctrine emerged and the specific meanings which were then attached to it, sovereignty reduces to a principle of political supremacy. The conventional definition of the sovereign state is a political unit in which the authorities have a monopoly of legal force. Wherever the claim to sovereign authority is successfully advanced there will generally be an attempt to disarm the population, or, failing that, to regulate by law the circumstances under which arms may be used by private citizens. In many societies the process of civilian pacification has been only imperfectly achieved, if at all. In no sovereign state, however, is there a formal toleration of private armies organised to protect interests and further aims other than those of the state itself. The monopoly of legal force is thus merely the means by which a government is able to enforce its claim to political supremacy. That claim entails an even more fundamental monopoly of domestic jurisdiction.

Within certain states, particularly the western democracies, the major political question has long been how to prevent the central authorities, i.e., those who control the state, from abusing their jurisdictional monopoly. Different ways of protecting the citizenry from its own government, even when democratically elected, have been devised in different countries, mostly involving the entrenchment of certain fundamental human rights and the creation of an independent judiciary. However, there are no states where the sovereignty of the individual within 'civil society' is considered absolute.

The familiar concept of a State of Emergency, during a war, provides sufficient support for this statement: for it is then, when normal civil rights may be suspended, when even a government which under normal circumstances regards the economy as predominantly the concern of private interests, will seek to control production, distribution and exchange, and will, if it is considered necessary for the war effort, requisition both economic resources and private property, that the principle of political supremacy is seen in its purist form.

The contemporary significance of this aspect of sovereignty will become apparent when we consider the implications for the state, and for international society, of shifting from a dynastic to a popular principle of legitimacy. The point to note here concerns the status of human rights. Locke had argued that, in addition to life and liberty, man had a natural right to property created or appropriated as a result of his own labour.[1] Whether any of these rights can be held to be 'naturally' inalienable is itself a contested question. But property rights clearly have the most dubious claim to that status. As a critic of natural law, J. S. Mill argued that property rights are a product of history, not of nature, and are thus ultimately always conventional and conditional.[2] They are conventional because the boundary separating the public from the private sphere (and every society *must* have some such boundary) is ultimately a question of custom and tacit social consent; they are conditional because what has been 'given' can always be taken away. In the end the distinction between civil society and the state, the drawing of which was one of the central tasks of western political theory from the seventeenth century onwards, leaves the principle of political supremacy intact.

The other aspect of the doctrine of sovereignty which is crucial for an understanding of its historical staying power, is its external face; or more accurately, the external consequences of the claim to political supremacy. In theory, the authority and power of a sovereign government over either its subjects or citizens is not limited by any higher or outside authority. Under international law any limitations must be voluntarily agreed. The orderly regulation of international relations requires that such limitations be negotiated according to the principle of *pacta sunt servanda* i.e., in the expectation that promises will be kept, but there is always an explicit codicil, namely, *rebus sic stantibus*, implying in effect the recognition that at the international level there is ultimately no authoritative legal mechanism for adjusting to change.

The sovereign monopoly of jurisdiction thus has two final requirements which we have already noted in the previous chapter: mutual recognition, without which it would be impossible to negotiate limitations at all; and legal equality, which is clearly definitional in a world which accepts the existence of more than one supreme authority. If the passions released by nationalist sentiment sometimes make it more difficult for states to honour the first of these requirements than in the traditional society of states, the rise of nationalism has made governments even more attached to the second. Even where common sense (and/or popular sentiment) might dictate otherwise, ethnic or national communities cannot easily opt for protectorate status. This is essentially because of the deeply held modern view that independence is a fundamental and inalienable human right.[3]

National self-determination

It is not possible to treat the principle of national self-determination in quite the same way as the principle of sovereignty. It is possible to argue about whether nations have always existed and there is certainly ample evidence to suggest that something approximating to national sentiment was mobilised by dynastic rulers in early modern Europe and elsewhere.[4] But for the principle of national self-determination to be advanced, it was necessary first for the concepts of the self, and self-determination, to be 'discovered' and then for these discoveries to seize the imagination of society at large.

The idea of self-determination is thus a product of a specifically *historical* consciousness. And this consciousness, which was eventually codified into the principle of popular sovereignty, did not develop overnight. According to José Ortega y Gasset, it was only in the aftermath of the First World War that it became firmly established, even in Europe. In *The Revolt of the Masses*, which was published in 1932, he describes the process in the following way (the self, it is true, is not mentioned but the whole argument clearly depends on its existence):

> In the 18th Century certain minority groups discovered that every human being, by the mere fact of birth, and without requiring any special qualification whatsoever, possessed certain fundamental political rights, the so-called rights of man and the citizen; and further that, strictly speaking, these rights, common to all, are the only ones that exist . . . This was at first a mere theory, the idea of a few men; then those few began to put the idea into practice, to impose it and insist upon it. Nevertheless, during the whole of the 19th Century, the mass, while gradually becoming enthusiastic to these rights as an ideal, did not feel them as rights, . . . the 'people' . . . had learned that it was sovereign but did not believe it. Today the ideal has been changed into a reality; not only in legislation, which is the mere framework of public life, but in the heart of every individual, whatever his ideas may be, and even if he be a reactionary in his ideas, *that is to say even when he attacks and castigates institutions by which those rights are sanctioned*.[5]

The abolition of the conceptual legitimacy of all privilege, first in theory and then in reality, was a momentous historical development, the final results of which are even now not fully determined. The unknown consequences are of both a practical and a theoretical kind. One of the practical consequences concerns the export of the egalitarian ideal beyond Europe. In many parts of the world this ideal has been eagerly embraced, as we shall see, but it is still not wholly believed. In their individual lives people are often still governed by their status within a traditional, if crumbling, prescriptive order, witness the residual, unofficial but still real political authority exercised by traditional rulers in parts of Africa or the pervasive influence of the caste system in India. What will happen in such countries, whose internal condition is already turbulent as the result of their having had to import the twentieth century from the west, as it were in packaged form, when such remnants of traditional society are finally stripped away?

For the moment, however, it is the unknown theoretical consequences of the new historical consciousness which have a more direct bearing on the argument. To reverse Ortega y Gasset's formulation, a question which is frequently asked, even by those who *support* the institutions by which fundamental rights are sanctioned is: where will it all stop? In other words, what is the correct definition and what are the natural boundaries of the 'People' whose rights were discovered in the eighteenth century?

This question does not have an unambiguous answer. It is perhaps best addressed via a short digression. It was not so long ago that women were regarded virtually everywhere as legally inferior to men, as they still are in several of the Swiss Cantons, let alone in much of Asia and Africa. And even where common rights have been acknowledged in theory as an ideal, social practice across the world suggests that the belief in the sovereignty of the people, that is all human beings, is rather less firmly established than Ortega y Gasset believed it to be in 1932. When Congresswoman Geraldine Ferraro was nominated in 1984 as the Democratic Party's Vice-Presidential candidate there was still a substantial minority in the United States, including women, who believed her to be disqualified because of her sex.[6] The experiment was not repeated in 1988.

The idea of female emancipation could clearly never have been formulated without the prior 'discovery' of fundamental human rights, since it was that discovery which was able to generate in turn the political goal of emancipation itself. But the boundary problem to which the concept of individual human rights inevitably gives rise does not stop there. The traditional defence for subordinating women to men was not that they did not possess fundamental rights but that, like children, criminals and lunatics, they were not fitted by nature or education or both to exercise them.

Few people perhaps will ever want to deny this proposition with respect to criminals or lunatics, although even here the ideal of egalitarian individualism notoriously undermines confidence in the conventional definitions of these two social categories. But in the case of children the undermining process is far more radical, since the age at which a child becomes capable of exercising his or her rights, once the stage of dependent infancy is passed, is clearly not fixed by nature. Is it to be the age when they are capable of earning their own living; or of bearing and fathering children of their own; or of being conscripted to die for their country? The answer to these questions can only be conventional and specific; it is impossible to arrive at any generally authoritative, ahistorical, context-free answer.

The point of the digression will now, I hope, be clear. It is this: that although the sovereignty of the people, and the conception of individual rights on which it is based, are essentially universal, i.e., they apply to all human beings or to none, the political claims to which they give rise are *always and necessarily* advanced by, or on behalf of, a particular group of people. They are also advanced in a specific context within which, it is held, their fundamental and universal human rights are being systematically withheld. This applies as much to the question of the proper constitution of the state itself as to the rights of all its members.

For, when all is said and done, what are these rights, which were discovered in the eighteenth century, after lying undisclosed through the ages under layer upon layer of privilege? In the most famous formulation they were life, liberty and the pursuit of happiness. And the greatest of these, at least in its ability to serve as an active political goal, without whose attainment the other rights must drop away, is undoubtedly liberty. 'One hardly knows', writes Mill, in the chapter from *Representative Government*[7] from which I have already quoted, 'what any division of the human race should be free to do if not to determine with which of the various collective bodies of human beings they choose to associate themselves.' There lay (and still lies) the rub. Just as to make sense of female emancipation one must assume *both* a collective identity of women as women separate from men *and* a political dispensation in which as women their fundamental rights are denied, so to make sense of the claim of national self-determination one must assume *both* a collective national identity *and* a state in which members of a particular nation have their fundamental rights similarly denied.

The doctrine of self-determination thus assumes that mankind is not merely divided according to gender but according to nationality; that this division is equally natural; that rule by foreigners therefore not only leads to 'natural' resentment but constitutes a denial of fundamental human rights; and that consequently each nation and no other entity has a right to constitute a separate state. Such reasoning is required if a theory of universal human rights is to be advanced as the justification for an independent political community. If it is accepted, there is no conflict between the doctrine of sovereignty and that of national self-determination: the one expresses a timeless political principle, the other the only historically relevant basis on which it should be exercised. As Alfred Cobban put it, after the French Revolution 'the theory of the Divine Right of Kings, which had been the chief political gospel of the early modern period . . . was replaced by the Divine Right of the People'; the people in other words stopped being subjects and became sovereign.

In practice the process was considerably less tidy and obvious than this reconciliation suggests. Both concepts are deeply ambiguous, a fact which arguably renders them politically rather than analytically powerful. Because of this ambiguity both are frequently contested in word and deed, on the grounds that they make claims which are contradicted by empirical evidence. The claim to sovereignty is ultimately a legal claim, which is advanced by one government and recognised by others; but if the claim departs too far from reality, as for example in contemporary Chad or the Lebanon, whose sovereign status seems to rely on little else than formal recognition; or, on the other side, in Rhodesia between 1965 and 1979 whose government was not recognised, but which exercised effective jurisdiction, at least in the early years of the rebellion, the doctrine will be ignored. The ambiguity of national self-determination is even more notorious. Sir Ivor Jennings summed up this ambiguity in 1956 in a famous remark concerning the United Nations debates on decolonisation. 'On the surface it seemed reasonable: let the People decide. It was in fact ridiculous because the people cannot decide until someone decides who are the people.'[8]

THE NEW POLITICAL MAP

There are some political concepts such as liberty, justice or even democracy itself, which are best regarded as 'essentially contested', that is to say, it is the political contest to define them authoritatively which constitutes their essence rather than any particular positive or empirical definition.[9] These concepts – and the nature of freedom is perhaps the most contested of all – are important because they have an enduring capacity to generate passionate and contradictory commitments. At any given time those who hold power will attempt to impose a particular set of definitions, for example, that

41

liberty should be understood as freedom from constraint under the law and should not be extended to include positive entitlements. Where the meaning of the concept is fundamentally ambiguous, however, they will seldom be successful for long.

Should the concept of national sovereignty be included in the list of (essentially contested) concepts? From one point of view one might argue not only that it should be included but that it is the paradigmatic contested concept: although the traditional view was that sovereignty could not be divided, a long succession of civil wars testifies to the fact that it can certainly be contested. In the twentieth century many such wars, for example the Nigerian Civil War and the war which led to the creation of Bangladesh in 1971, have been fought over the alleged denial of the right of national self-determination to groups which feel themselves disenfranchised within the existing state structure.

Yet from another point of view the answer is not so clear. Short of the millennium, it is impossible to imagine general agreement on the positive content of justice. It is similarly improbable that the tension between liberty and equality will ever be resolved. On the other hand, it is difficult but not impossible to conceive of a time when the problem of 'constitutional' order throughout the world could be resolved.* Indeed it is precisely because liberty and equality are perceived as *essentially* contested concepts, while constitutional order can in principle be defined on the basis of consent, that within open societies greater emphasis is placed on procedure than on substance, that is, on the rules governing political competition. Such rules must be both public and transparent.

Practice seldom conforms very closely to theory and liberal societies have always been in the minority. Yet the process whereby nationalism (and the doctrine of national self-determination which it spawned), helped to re-shape the political map of the world, would be unintelligible without reference to the world-wide appeal of the ideal of a legitimate 'free' state.[10] A free state is one in which the question of its physical existence and constitutional order have been put beyond question whatever political disputes may persist internally.

I suggest, therefore, that the creation of states during the nationalist era must be viewed as an integral part of the history of liberty. As Benedetto Croce wrote, liberty is 'on the one hand the explanatory principle of the course of history, and, on the other, the moral ideal of

---

* In practice, secession, which draws its moral force from its popular basis, is a standing challenge to the Society of States as at present constituted. (See chapter 4.) But the diffusion of constitutional arrangements, which would translate consent into government world-wide, is not itself unthinkable.

humanity'.[11] By this he did not mean that the story moved, by a series of preconceived steps in a straight line towards its inevitable end, but that the ideal of liberty provided the only measure against which to record the compromises, setbacks and disasters as much as the triumphs, victories and heroic deeds of mankind. It is the ideal, in other words, which makes it possible to tell a story at all. In the case before us the story appears to have unfolded in a dialectical movement.

The break-up of the European multi-national empires

The diffusion of nationalist doctrine, that is, the deliberate exploitation of national and/or ethnic sentiment for political ends, is generally viewed by historians as part of the reaction to Napoleon's invasions. The nationalist reaction started in Germany and Italy and spread eastwards. The principles of the Revolution of 1789 had been couched in universal language (that was and remains their appeal); now they were nationalised and put at the service of a specifically French imperial order.[12] Not surprisingly, therefore, the constitutional and republican reaction to Napoleon also took a national form. The principles of the revolution had been betrayed. Although their re-demption certainly involved the reassertion that they belonged to mankind, and not merely to France, they could only be redeemed in practice in the territories which had been subordinated to French imperial rule, and where, after the defeat of Napoleon, the *ancien régime* had been restored and defended by the creation of the Holy Alliance between Russia, Prussia and Austria.

The first sustained attempt to break this old-new order failed in 1848. I am not concerned with retelling this familiar story, nor indeed with charting the course of the popular and constitutional principles of the revolution during the remainder of the nineteenth century. It is sufficient for the argument to make two observations about this period. The first is that the opponents of reaction, and of the dynastic principle on which it was based, were constitutionalists, intellectuals who had accepted the universal ideals of the Enlightenment and the revolution. Secondly, to parody Pirendello, they were for the most part characters in search of a constituency. Political leaders who wish to establish their right to lead, on the basis of the principle of self-determination and popular sovereignty, must obviously appeal to a sentiment of group identity and loyalty. And where it does not already exist or is only latent, they may even have to create it.[13]

Thus was the marriage between liberalism and nationalism effected.

43

The process was begun whereby the generally austere, classical and unashamedly elitist universalism of the Enlightenment, was transformed into the warmer and culturally and historically specific language of political romanticism. From the constitutional haven of England, Mill could allow himself to be influenced by Coleridge into endorsing nationalism, in part for instrumental reasons – he believed that 'free institutions are next to impossible in a country made up of different nationalities'.[14] It seems unlikely that for those involved in the political struggle east of the Rhine, the implied tension between constitutionalism and nationalism would have been readily apparent.

Historically, the achievement of nineteenth-century liberal nationalists was to have kept alive the ideal of popular sovereignty as the basis for state creation until circumstances, mostly created by forces beyond their control, allowed them to influence the new political dispensation. At the Versailles Peace Conference in 1918, President Woodrow Wilson of the United States failed to dictate the terms of the peace, but not even his sternest critics would deny that he had an enormous influence on its general shape.

Wilson made the principle of national self-determination the basis of his plan for a new international order. In his mind there was no gap between national self-determination and democracy (for what other purpose would a people claim the right to self-determination if not to rule themselves?) and between both these concepts and the idea of a self-policing system of collective security to replace the discredited system of international power politics (for if all legitimate national and democratic aspirations had been met would not all have a joint interest in deterring any disturbance of the peace?).

Notoriously, the central problem with this vision on which the League of Nations was based, lay in its failure to confront the problem of power as an enduring reality rather than as an anachronistic feature of the old order. But, the implementation of the plan also confronted immediate problems of a more practical nature. These difficulties can be summed up in a word: minorities. To take just one example, from amongst those cited by Alfred Cobban in his study of *National Self-Determination*, that of Alsace-Lorraine between 1871 and 1910: 'about half-a-million French had left the conquered provinces . . . and some three hundred thousand Germans had come to take their place'.[15] In such circumstances what was the population group which was to be given the right of national self-determination?

Once an attempt is made to rule out conquest as a legitimate means of acquiring political rights, this kind of practical difficulty assumes much more than merely historical significance. In human affairs there

44

can be no such thing as a *tabula rasa*: however the political map is re-drawn, there are going to be dissatisfied groups. It is the recognition of this stubborn fact, which has produced, at the international level, the pragmatic reconciliation between the prescriptive principle of state sovereignty and the popular principle of national self-determination.

I shall return to this reconciliation in the final section of this chapter; for the moment it is important to recognise, not the practical dilemmas posed by the Wilsonian scheme but its triumphant success, both at the imaginative level and in terms of political organisation. After 1918 the dominant political form was the nation-state rather than the multi-national empire. The days of coexistence between popular sovereignty and dynasticism were numbered. The European imperial powers, particularly Britain and France, may have attempted to outwit the American president whenever they thought it necessary to protect their state patrimony, both close to home and further afield, but in the end they had nothing to put in the place of national self-determination as an ordering principle for international society.[16]

National sentiment and liberal imperialism

It is a major paradox in the history of national self-determination that the struggle for political liberty in Europe coincided with the expansion of European power to every corner of the globe. The most powerful imperialists, Britain and France, were also the countries in which liberal constitutionalism was most securely anchored and where national unification had proceeded furthest. Attempts to unravel this paradox have led some to view nineteenth-century imperialism as a form of expansionist nationalism, and others to see nationalism as a mere epi-phenomenon and to seek the explanation in the internal dynamics and structure of western capitalism. A powerful argument can be advanced on both sides but to follow the dispute it would be necessary to return to the quagmire of causal explanations. Since the rival protagonists start from incompatible premises, it seems safe for the observer to conclude that the dispute will never be resolved.

By contrast, the consequences of liberal imperialism for the re-ordering of international society on the basis of national self-determination seem relatively clear. From the start there was a contradiction between the political values of liberal democracy and the idea of a nationally, and ultimately racially, defined imperial order. This contradiction could be resolved, at least in the minds of liberal imperialists, so long as it was still possible to conceive of the world as divided between civilised powers and barbarians. But since liberal values were ultimately grounded in the Enlightenment discovery of universal human rights, this distinction could no longer be regarded as part of the natural order. Consequently, it was necessary to envisage a process whereby barbarian states could graduate into 'civilised' international society after a period of enlightened education and preparation for self-government.[17]

In practice, this meant that the ultimate ideological justification of liberal empire was that it should preside over its own eventual elimination. Of course the period of tutelage, an idea to which liberal imperialists were often attracted, could stretch far into the future. After the Second World War the British continued to recruit young men on the assumption that the colonial service still offered a lifetime career. But once their own arguments, i.e. those of liberal democracy, were turned against them by Asian and African nationalists, the liberal imperialist powers had no secure defence.[18] They did not, it is true, give up without a struggle, or at least without complaint; and they were not short of self-interested reasons which allowed them to delay the day of reckoning. But the Achilles' heel of liberal empire was not the relegation of Britain and France in the international power political league; it was the cognitive scheme and political values on which liberalism itself was based. In other words, all they could do was play for time.

The evidence for this claim – and I am not talking here about some deep structural cancer in the body of liberal imperial thought, but of its half-conscious recognition by those who saw themselves as representing 'civilisation' – is to be found in the creation of the League of Nations Mandate system.[19] This system is often represented as a typical piece of liberal hypocrisy: a way by which the victorious allies parcelled out amongst themselves Germany's overseas colonies and the Levantine provinces of the Ottoman Empire, as part of a Carthaginian peace, while pretending to do something else. On this view, indeed, it was little more than the continuation of the scramble for Africa by other means.

So far as it goes, there is nothing wrong with this interpretation: the victorious powers did indeed divide Germany's colonies amongst themselves and absorbed them within their own empires. From an administrative point of view, it mattered little whether a colony had been originally established by Britain or France, or whether it had been taken over as a going concern from Germany: it remained a colony. At the peace conference the imperial powers refused to contemplate applying the principle of national self-determination beyond Europe.

The problem with this conventional interpretation is that it does not go far enough. By creating a special category of colonies for whose administration, in theory, they were to be accountable to the international community, and by sub-dividing this category according to the prospects of particular territories for self-government, and by designating even the most backward as 'a sacred trust for civilisation', the liberal imperialists had, in effect, made the first public admission that empire in and of itself was no longer a legitimate political form.

After 1919, first in the Middle East, then in Asia and finally in Africa, the full significance of this admission was recognised and exploited by anti-colonial nationalists. But even if it was feasible for the imperial powers to argue that the Ottoman territories were in a special category, what was the essential difference in terms of fundamental human rights between these territories and those which made up Britain's Indian Empire? And how could one possibly argue that the Tanganyikans or the Togolese would ultimately be able to exercise their right of national self-determination, because they were citizens of mandated territories, while those of the Gold or Ivory Coasts, or Kenya, would not? Once decolonisation became a major international issue, the new nationalists were able to call in aid the fifth column of liberal opinion within the metropolitan countries themselves.

But the collusion between metropolitan centre and colonial periphery went even further than this formulation suggests: while, within the metropole, the fifth column was led by anti-colonial activists, the nationalists were ultimately effective because they were pushing against an already open door.

Ortega y Gasset was right in his diagnosis of mass society: the eighteenth-century idea of the rights of man and the citizen had finally taken hold of the deep political beliefs even of those who 'attack and castigate the institutions by which these rights are sanctioned'. Wherever this statement did not apply, there the progress of decolonisation was halted. Before 1974 the Portuguese did not enjoy either political or civil rights and there was no basis, therefore, for an alliance between nationalists in Angola, Mozambique and Guinea-Bissau and liberal opinion in Portugal. An alliance was, of course, formed between the nationalists and the Portuguese communists, but until the revolution it operated in the political underworld, since both the Portuguese communist party and the African nationalist parties were banned.

47

Anti-colonial nationalism

In one recent study it has been suggested that anti-colonialism was only one manifestation of a more fundamental modern quest for autonomy. In this period of human history, Dov Ronen writes:

> The cardinal element has not been man's aspiration to find his identity in, or to become part of, a nation, but rather the individual human beings aspiration to control his own life, to realise his or her right to self-determination. To do this, individuals assumed at times a national identity, at other times a class, minority or racial identity. This assumed identity has been correlated with the perceived identity of the obstacles to aspirations: Napoleon and the France that he represented seemed the obstacle to the Germans, the capitalist owner of private property to the proletariat, the oppressive majority to East European nationalities, and white colonialism to African and Asian peoples.[20]

Theoretically, this formulation is undoubtedly attractive. The problem with the concept of self-determination is that it is impossible to provide a coherent account of the self in isolation from some wider social group; and the problem with applying the concept of a nation to many Asian and African states is that culturally they are highly heterogeneous.

As a description of practice, Ronen's argument is less persuasive. While it is true that the anti-colonial struggle was almost invariably a struggle to capture the colonial state, very often in the absence of popular national sentiment, anti-colonial leaders always claimed to be representing an existing nation or creating a movement whose historical task was to bring one into being. Their appeal to the principle of national self-determination may have been fortuitous, in the sense that it was available both intellectually and, as one of the principles on which the United Nations Charter was based, in an institutionalised form. But as a route to independence it was spectacularly successful. In a period of little more than twenty years it led to the creation of more than one hundred new states all of which claimed to uphold the principle.

The impact of anti-colonial nationalism on international society appears at first sight to have been both wide-ranging and subversive. With the support of the Soviet Union and its allies, the loose alliance of Afro-Asian states had, by 1960, succeeded in de-legitimising the concept of colonial empire. Under General Assembly Resolution 1514[21] not only was the possession of colonies condemned, but the lack of preparation for self-government was ruled out as a defence for delaying the 'granting of independence to those territories that remained under colonial rule.

The new states were also very largely responsible for lengthening the traditional agenda of international relations. Their preoccupation with economic development, and their long campaign, at the United Nations and elsewhere, to create a new economic order under which power and wealth would be more equitably distributed was in large part the continuation of anti-colonial nationalism by other means.

It is not difficult to understand this phenomenon, which is discussed more fully in chapter 7. The point to note here is that anti-colonial nationalism was essentially reactive. The nationalist leaders more often than not mobilised diverse groups who shared a hostility to colonial rule rather than a pre-colonial group sentiment or identity of interest. In the aftermath of independence many of the new leaders faced a crisis of legitimacy: political control was now in their hands, yet they were seldom able either to redeem the broad promises they had made to bring about the rapid social and economic transformation of society, or more specifically, to satisfy all the sub-national interests whose competition for state largesse now dominated the political arena. Since the colonial economy substantially survived the transfer of power, the international campaign for economic independence, which as with the earlier political struggle was supported by liberal opinion in the west, was thus at the same time a means of maintaining the nationalist credentials of the successor regime and, it was hoped, a strategy for securing the modernisation of post-colonial societies.

But, if in relation to the industrial west anti-colonial nationalists have continued to advance their revisionist demands, in relation to other post-colonial states they have opted for an *étatism* which is both traditional and unyielding. Indeed, from this point of view, it is the traditional society of states which has had the greater impact on anti-colonial nationalism rather than the other way round. By facilitating the creation of new states, the principle of national self-determination, in effect, guaranteed its own metamorphosis. A marriage was arranged between the popular and prescriptive principles of sovereignty, on terms which were very disadvantageous to the former. The new states turned out to be as unsympathetic to demands for self-determination from dissatisfied groups within their jurisdiction as were the Romanov, Habsburg and Ottoman rulers to the national claims that were advanced against their rule in the nineteenth century. The reasons behind this transformation of the principle of national self-determination and the permanent challenge which it poses to international society are the subjects of the next chapter.

4 NATIONALISM AND THE INTERNATIONAL ORDER

Ostensibly, the world has been made safe for nationalism, the hierarchy of the traditional dynastic world giving way everywhere before the permissive and popular principle of national self-determination. The reality is considerably more complex. Much as the early Christian church was once captured and tamed by an institutionalised clerisy, so in the twentieth century the new civil religion of the nation has been captured and modified by the institutional order of the already existing society of states. Indeed, the analogy might usefully be extended further: just as religious enthusiasm, the subversive appeal of a return to the true faith, has always lain beneath the orthodoxies of the Christian churches, and has from time to time broken out in open challenge to established religion, so, as we shall see, the ideal of 'true' popular national sovereignty has never been wholly domesticated. Before attempting to assess the challenge which it poses for the established international order it is worth considering in more detail why this process of domestication occurred and the particular form that it took.

THE DOMESTICATION OF NATIONAL SELF-DETERMINATION

The process began almost as soon as national self-determination was advanced as the new principle of international legitimacy after 1918. It involved, first, equating the popular principle of sovereignty with the attack on the remaining dynastic empires in Europe, and later with anti-colonialism generally. Secondly, it involved abandoning the constitutional mode of settling disputed claims in favour of political settlements.

Not surprisingly, groups whose political self-consciousness developed after the break-up of the old empires have viewed the attempted taming of national self-determination with dismay, seeing it as a betrayal of the progressive ideal, and as a victory for reaction.

50

Unhappily, no such easy judgement is defensible. Whatever the particular reasons why self-proclaimed national groups have continued to challenge the authority of the state (and seem likely to do so for the foreseeable future), the ultimate explanation for the partial surrender of the doctrine of popular sovereignty does not lie in human cowardice but in the indeterminacy of the concept of the collective self. The power of the concept rests on the empirical observation that men live (and always have lived) in groups, and the virtual impossibility of conceiving circumstances in which they would not do so. The indeterminacy arises because the boundaries of the collective are not given by nature. Individuals are ultimately bounded by their physical being, but although romantic nationalists have often tried to argue otherwise, there are no national boundaries defining the collective self.

Criteria and agenda

It will, no doubt, be objected that there is nothing indeterminate about the idea of collective identity from an existential standpoint. A group, let us say the Kurds or the Eritreans, which can command heroic sacrifices and unquestioning loyalty (and loyalty and a willingness to make the ultimate sacrifice are clearly very closely related even if they are not synonymous) has surely passed the only *conceivable* test. To quote J. S. Mill again: 'One hardly knows what any division of the human race should be free to do if not to determine with which of the various collective bodies of human beings they choose to associate themselves.'[1]

But this defence will not work. At least it will not work so long as we wish to avoid returning to the world of brutal realism. Mill appears to believe that the collective divisions of mankind are given unambigously by nature and history. It is, presumably, this belief which allows him to accommodate self-determination to the nationality principle. But, if we accept that history, unlike nature, cannot be assumed to exist independently of our consciousness, then there is no escaping the existential conclusion. This is that the nation is ultimately a group whose identity is forged by a particular interpretation of its own history. Thus fortified, the 'nation' is in a position to take on the world, daring the authorities to deny its existence by suppressing it by force.

The ultimate, pathological, version of this view of the collective self was provided by the Third Reich whose public philosophy both glorified the role of force in securing the triumph of the will, and was openly disdainful of any concept of international order. But if National Socialism was the perverted, pathological version, how should we

51

conceive of the norm, or establish criteria for adjudicating between the claims of rival groups to constitute a legitimate collective self?

Once it is acknowledged that no external objective criteria exist for distinguishing between legitimate and illegitimate collectives, or between real and false nations, then at first sight the plebiscite (an open test of public opinion designed to solicit the wishes of individuals with regard to their collective identity), appears to have much to recommend it. This was, indeed, the technique initially favoured by Wilsonian liberals at the time of the Versailles Conference.

As a method for establishing that the right of national self-determination has been exercised the plebiscite has two obvious weaknesses. First, it assumes that a collective identity already exists – otherwise, who or what would decide which people to poll; secondly, it discounts the agenda problem – that is the problem which arises because of the fact that whoever controls the questions on which a particular population is to be asked to vote, is in a very strong position also to control the outcome.

Perhaps these formidable weaknesses were not immediately obvious to optimistic liberals at the end of the First World War.[2] But they quickly became so as the powers set about redrawing the political map of Europe. Their exposure occurred within a specific historical context and in three overlapping kinds of situation. It has since become clear that these situations are likely to arise wherever the plebiscite is used to settle a question of self-determination.

There is first and most fundamentally the problem of minorities. In the course of their history the 'nationalities' of Europe had been hopelessly scrambled, so that even assuming that each could have been assigned a national territory there would have been many nationals left outside, unless the aftermath of the plebiscite was to involve major involuntary population movements. This possibility dramatises the agenda problem: for what kind of self-determination is it that requires people, who may have been settled in one place for generations, and many of whom will be very young or very old, either to uproot themselves or to forfeit their political rights?

Secondly, there is the question of territory. In the pre-nationalist society of states it had been possible for a title to land to be acquired by conquest, as for example Quebec was acquired by Britain under the Treaty of Paris in 1763. In the modern idiom what this appears to mean is that a right could derive from a wrong; that in time possession would not be nine-tenths of the law but the law itself. However, once subjects were converted into citizens, and dynastic into popular sovereignty, their ancestral homeland became, in a conceptual sense, inalienable. Since all old states had been formed by conquest, and it was clearly impossible to redeem the wrongs of history *in toto*, the immediate question concerned the cut-off dates. In other words, where was the line to be drawn between the old dispensation and the new?

As we saw in chapter 4, one consequence of the Franco-Prussian war was a substantial French emigration from and German immigration into Alsace-Lorraine. In these circumstances the French government feared that if the people were given a choice between incorporation in France or Germany (independence was not considered seriously as an option) the vote might be insufficiently conclusive in favour of France. They therefore opposed settling the future of the disputed territory by plebiscite and insisted, retroactively, on the illegitimacy of the German occupation of 1871.[3]

Finally, there is the intractable problem of state integrity and security. The victorious powers were willing to contemplate using the plebiscite as a technique for deciding the basis of new states, but they did not want it applied to themselves or to their possessions. The British were in general more enthusiastic than the French about its possibilities in the European context, but they had no intention of settling the Irish question by plebiscite, let alone allowing its use in India or their other imperial possessions. Such attitudes established the general pattern for the future. Although the plebiscite has survived and was used by the United Nations as a way of settling the fate of the former mandated territories of Togo and the Cameroons, which had been divided between the British and the French after the First World War and were transformed to the United Nations Trusteeship Council after the Second, it has been increasingly pushed into the margins of discussion of national self-determination, in favour of strategic and political criteria.

The Kashmir dispute[4] provides a more recent example of why such marginalisation occurs. The formula under which the fate of the princely states was decided at the time of Britain's partition of India in 1947 – i.e. the rulers were allowed to opt for either India or Pakistan – enabled the Hindu ruling dynasty to opt for India despite the fact that Kashmir physically abutted on to West Pakistan and that the overwhelming majority of its population was Muslim. When Pakistan infiltrated 'volunteers' across the frontier claiming a spontaneous uprising against the Maharajah's decision in favour of India, the government of India promptly referred the dispute to the Security Council.

The major powers refused to accept the Indian argument that

Pakistan had committed an aggression and should therefore be forced to withdraw from Kashmir, if necessary by the use of sanctions under Chapter 7 of the Charter. They did so partly because they saw merit in the Pakistani view that the Maharajah's decision, while legally within his rights, constituted a breach of 'natural justice'. In the course of the diplomacy which led finally to the *de facto* partition of the state, the Indian government offered to conduct a plebiscite once the situation had stabilised. By this they presumably meant once they were satisfied that Pakistan was not in a position to determine the outcome. In any event, while the government's formal commitment to a plebiscite was never revoked, it quickly became clear that since India could not control the outcome itself, and since Pakistan would not withdraw from 'Azad' (free) Kashmir without a test of opinion, the Indians were unlikely to honour the commitment in practice. To have done so would have been politically unpopular in India at any time. After the Sino-Indian War of 1962, in which Pakistan had been openly sympathetic to the Chinese, the Indian government also believed it would have been strategically unwise.

From the League to the United Nations

The Kashmir dispute repeated the major lesson that had been learned from earlier attempts to use the plebiscite in support of national self-determination, namely that it is impossible to prevent the intrusion of the political and strategic interests of the major powers. The pragmatic solution adopted after the First World War involved using the language of national self-determination but re-drawing the map of Europe so that it roughly reflected the nationality principle but without any fixed procedure and subject to considerations of practicality and political interest.

The trouble with this approach, as Alfred Cobban pointed out, was that it created the political problem of minorities and removed the principle of nationality from the realm of choice to that of nature or essence, substituting the idea of national determinism for the idea of an act of self-determination.[5] Woodrow Wilson was aware of the potential for tyranny which this adaptation of the principle involved. He tried to guard against it in his original version of Article X of the League Covenant. Since this represents the last attempt to provide a mechanism for peaceful territorial revision in the international system, and so to reconcile the libertarian ideal with political reality, it is worth quoting in full:

> The contracting powers unite in guaranteeing to each other political independence and territorial integrity; but it is understood between

54

them that such territorial adjustments, if any, as may in the future become necessary by reason of changes in present racial conditions and aspirations or present social and political relationships, pursuant to the principle of self-determination, and also such territorial readjustments as may in the judgment of three-fourths of the Delegates be demanded by the welfare and manifest interests of the people concerned, may be effected, if agreeable to those peoples.[6]

Such a radical departure from the principle of state sovereignty did not survive the scrutiny even of the American delegation to the Peace Conference let alone those of the European powers. The protection of national minorities under the League proved ineffective, and the concept of minority rights fell further into disrepute after Hitler had justified his assaults on Austria and Czechoslovakia in terms of the right of self-determination for their German-speaking populations. Against this background, it was not surprising that when it came to drafting the United Nations Charter, the powers were anxious to play down the issue of cultural nationalism in the interests of obtaining cooperation between states whose territorial integrity was collectively guaranteed.

The conventional interpretation

After 1945, despite the obeisance paid to the principle of national self-determination in the Charter, wherever nations came into conflict with the state, it was the people who had to move. Starting in Europe, where 10 million Germans were uprooted in the aftermath of the war, and continuing with the mass population transfers that accompanied the partition of India, hardly a year has passed without some group of people being caught in the cross-fire of political conflict and driven from their homes. The refugee column, that bedraggled snake of people fleeing for their lives with only such possessions as they can carry or bundle on to hand-carts and pack-animals, has become an all too typical emblem of the twentieth century. By the 1980s Africa alone, the last continent to be decolonised with some fifty new 'nation-states replacing the European colonies, had a population of over 5 million refugees, an estimated one-half of the world's total.

Evidently, the contemporary interpretation of national self-determination is highly conventional: in effect its application has been tied in time and space to the withdrawal of the European powers from their overseas possessions. This formulation has been enthusiastically accepted by the African and Asian successor states. Thus in 1961 Jawaharlal Nehru finally overcame his scruples about political violence and sanctioned the forceful incorporation of Goa into India without reference to Goan opinion.[7] And in 1967, after the inhabitants of Gibraltar had voted overwhelmingly to maintain the *status quo* – in a 97 per cent poll there were only 44 dissenters – the United Nations Committee on Colonialism ruled that British rule was a violation of the Charter because the inhabitants were not indigenous.[8]

Post-colonial tests of public opinion as a means of settling disputes over self-determination have also been ruled out by the regional organisations that were set up by the Asian and African states after independence. In Africa, where before independence nationalists had talked of the necessity of revising the 'artificial' boundaries which had been drawn up by the European powers in the nineteenth century, the unnegotiable acceptance of the territorial *status quo* turned out to be one of the two crucial supports of the Organisation of African Unity (OAU) when it was established in 1963. The other was the equally unnegotiable commitment to support the liberation of the remaining colonial territories whether they were ruled directly from Europe, or, as in Rhodesia and South Africa, by European minorities.

When, after military defeat by Ethiopia in 1978, Somalia revised its constitution, replacing the commitment to reunite all Somali-speaking peoples within one state by a commitment to support colonial people struggling against oppression, the other members of the OAU remained notably unimpressed.[9] In other words, in terms of the conventional interpretation, South Africa was a legitimate target of anti-colonial nationalism, despite the fact that it had been an independent state since 1910, whereas the Ethiopian Empire was not, despite the fact that the Amharic ascendency had been extended as a result of Emperor Menelik's involvement with the European powers in the scramble for Africa.

The historical fate of the principle of national self-determination is doubly ironic: it has conquered the world for the people by legitimising the state and only the state, which claims to speak in their name; and it has elevated and institutionalised the progressive view of human affairs by attempting to freeze the political map in a way which has never previously been attempted. Intuitively, this unprecedented attempt to bring history to an end, at least so far as the territorial division of the world is concerned, seems unlikely to succeed, at least so long as in other respects the world continues to be dominated by historical thinking and historical consciousness.

Yet, for the most part, it must be admitted, nationalist movements have not been very successful in overthrowing the conventional interpretation of national self-determination as a once and for all event in the past. Two questions therefore arise: first what kinds of challenge does nationalism – a doctrine which depends on the development of historical consciousness and identity – pose for the contemporary international order; second, under what kinds of circumstances is this challenge likely to be successful? I shall consider these questions in turn.

TWO CHALLENGES

The most that can be said for the conventional (i.e. anti-colonial) interpretation of national self-determination is that it is a sensible compromise. Given the indeterminacy of the idea of the collective self on the one hand, and the impossibility within the contemporary stock of political ideas of arriving at an alternative justification of political authority on the other, it represents some kind of deal, albeit a somewhat shabby one, between the entrenched forces of liberal rationalism and those of historical essentialism. Like all compromises, sensible though they may seem to the practical men who negotiate them, the conventional interpretation of national self-determination remains vulnerable to attack from those who believe that the compromisers have misunderstood either the essential nature of their historical claim or its essential rationality. Although there are many points where the two aspects overlap, it may be helpful, if only for presentational purposes, to identify the main essentialist challenge to the international order with irridentism and the main rationalist challenge with secession.

Irridentism

The doctrine of irridentism is derived from the Italian, *irridenta*, meaning those territories, Trente, Dalmatia, Trieste, Fiume which although culturally Italian remained under Austrian or Swiss rule and thus *unredeemed* after the unification of Italy itself. In modern political usage the term has come to mean any territorial claim made by one sovereign national state to lands within another. These claims are generally supported by historical and/or ethnic arguments: that is, the irridentist state insists that part of its rightful homeland has been unjustly taken from it, or that a part of the nation itself has been falsely separated from the organic national community.

Although, in all cases, irridentist claims are made by one state on the territory (the real estate so to speak) of another, irridentist claims vary, nonetheless, in the extent to which they combine the elements of

57

territoriality for its own sake and genuine national sentiment. A current if extreme example was provided by the Argentine claim to the Malvinas or Falkland Islands which has been deliberately kept in the forefront of the Argentine national consciousness by the process of official national propaganda and censorship. All Argentinian maps show the islands as belonging to the Argentine. Argentinian history books describe them as an integral part of the nation, despite the fact that there has been virtually no Argentinian population on the islands for 150 years and not much before that.[10]

An example of irridentism, where a claim to territory was combined with arguments about the allegiance of the population, is provided by the Moroccan claim to Mauritania in the early 1960s. As with the Argentine's claim to the Falklands/Malvinas, the Moroccan claim was historical. In this case the claim was based on the overlordship or suzerainty which the Moroccan sultans had exercised over the peoples of Mauritania before the establishment of the French Empire in West Africa and the French protectorate over Morocco itself.[11] What gave the claim its salience in the politics of contemporary Morocco was the fact that the vision of a greater Morocco was shared by the ruling dynasty and by the Istiqlal, the nationalist part which in most other respects was in opposition to the regime. In this case irridentism opened up a prospect of a bipartisan foreign policy.

Two politically more ambiguous examples of modern irridentism are provided by the Spanish claim to Gibraltar on historical and geo-political grounds, and the Republic of Ireland's commitment to a united Ireland. Given the historical consciousness of the Spanish and Irish people (whether it is true or false is not here in question) and consequently their latent national consciousness (i.e. it is always available for political mobilisation) it seems unlikely that any Spanish or Irish government would be able to abandon their claims altogether. At the same time, in neither country is the irridentist question a major national issue, and indeed it is very often an embarrassment to the authorities.[12]

The Spanish claim is embarrassing because, given the expressed wishes of the population of Gibraltar on the one hand, and the Spanish government's accession into the EEC and its desire to integrate itself into the Western Alliance on the other, the claim, and the friction it engenders, inevitably seem anachronistic. By contrast, the Irish commitment to unity is embarrassing because the Irish government is heir to the partition agreement which established the Republic as an independent state. The Irish government knows that if it were to honour its commitment to unification, it would, even on the most optimistic assumptions, have to underwrite a different social order in the north, including secular education and welfare services of a kind which are not available in the Republic. On probably more realistic assumptions, it would find itself saddled with a civil war in the north which could well spread to the south and threaten its legitimacy. As yet no solution to the Irish question is in sight, and all recent Irish governments have consequently preferred the *status quo*.

These examples of modern irridentism, in which claims to land and appeals to popular sentiment are conjoined, suggest a general feature of irridentist claims. Since they are mostly claims by what may loosely be called the national core, which already has its own independent government, to peripheral lands (with or without the allegiance of their populations), they are available to governments as a mobilisation instrument, a means of securing popular support at times when, for whatever reason, such support seems particularly desirable.

Of course there are risks involved in cynically playing the irridentist card. If, as the Argentinian Junta discovered, a government is capable of arousing national dreams but cannot deliver what it promises, it may not be forgiven. Its successor will be left with the unpalatable task of containing the irridentist passion without disowning the claim. But while playing the irridentist card is likely to have unforeseen consequences, it remains broadly true that pressing an irridentist claim, where one is available, is an option which governments can choose to exercise. It is a way of tapping the well-springs of popular support even if, having switched the tap on at will, it cannot always be turned off.

The PLO, an organization without a territory or a state, is a spectacular exception to this rule. So long as it had no realistic chance of securing an independent state of Palestine, its irridentism was unequivocal, covering the entire state of modern Israel. Yasser Arafat's public acknowledgement of Israel's right to exist, made before the United Nations General Assembly in December 1988, has created a new political context. If the PLO is to have any chance of capitalising on this new situation, it will have to dilute the claim by deliberate use of ambiguity. In other words, it will have to behave more like an established irridentist government, for whom pressing its claim is a policy option rather than an ideological imperative. Whether the leadership of the organization will be allowed, by its own internal critics and its opponents in Israel, to act in this way remains to be seen.

The case which most clearly demonstrates the rule is also an exception to it. In 1960 the Republic of Somalia came into being as a result of a union of the British and Italian Trust territories. From its inception the new state had an irridentist constitution: the national flag was a five-pointed star, each point symbolising a centre of Somali population, only two of which were contained within the Republic. The other three centres were in Djibouti on the Red Sea, in the North-Eastern province of Kenya and in the Ogaden region of Ethiopia. Under their constitution Somali governments were committed to work for reunification.[13]

What makes Somali irridentism exceptional is first the fact that, uniquely in Africa, national sentiment is a mass rather than an elite phenomenon, and secondly that the Somali clan which has dominated the government in Mogadishu for most of the period since independence has extensive kinship links with the population living in the Ogaden. The combination of these two factors has kept unification as the dominant theme of Somali politics from the beginning, and has consequently isolated Somalia from its neighbours. Somali irridentism led to a defence treaty between Ethiopia and Kenya which survived both the 1974 revolution in Ethiopia and the United States negotiation of facilities for its Rapid Deployment Forces with Somalia and Kenya, and attempts to align the two regimes against 'Marxist' Ethiopia.[14]

Nevertheless, between 1969, when Siad Barre ousted the civilian government in a military *coup d'état*, and 1977, when he finally expelled his Russian allies and attempted unsuccessfully to take the Ogaden by force, his government endeavoured to conform to the general pattern. There is no evidence to suggest that the Russians, with whom the Somalis negotiated a friendship treaty involving extensive military and civilian aid in return for naval facilities for the Soviet forces, ever encouraged the government to press their territorial claim. And indeed for much of this period Barre's policy was publicly aimed at bringing about substantial change in the character of Somali society. His attempt at a revolution from above involved him in deliberately attempting to relocate many Northern nomads in the South as settled agriculturalists. It also involved censoring popular music on Somali radio: the oral tradition of Somali poetry, translated into a modern musical idiom adapted for the transistor age, was a vehicle for an alternative and irridentist form of political mobilisation.

It was only after the Ethiopian revolution had led to the general collapse of central authority and a revival of separatist sentiment throughout the country (not just in the Ogaden) that a combination of external opportunity – the Russian support for the revolution made a reversal of alliances seem plausible – and popular disaffection with his economic policies, led Siad Barre to embark on his disastrous policy of supporting the West Somali Liberation Front (WSLF) with regular and irregular military forces from within Somalia itself. The change in the Somali constitution after the country's defeat in 1978 was an attempt once again to bring popular irridentist sentiment firmly under the control of the central government.

Secession

The second challenge to the orthodox interpretation of self-determination as a once and for all event, secession, is, in a sense, a mirror image of the irridentist challenge. Successful secession is very rare; the creation of the state of Bangladesh in 1971 is the only pure example since 1945. However, the term is also used to describe unsuccessful separatist rebellions against the state. Indeed it is frequently used to describe any attempt by a national minority to exercise its right to self-determination by breaking away either to join another state or more often to establish an independent state of its own, or at least an autonomous region within an existing state. Such attempts are sometimes outright bids for independence, as when Biafra tried to secede from the Nigerian Federation between 1967 and 1970, or in the continuing Eritrean struggle against its incorporation in Ethiopia. On other occasions, as in Southern Sudan, Baluchistan or among the Sikhs of the Punjab, they are contests in which the options of national autonomy within the state or independence are both kept deliberately open.

But if tactical calculations of this kind are an integral part of secessionist as of irridentist politics, there is one vital difference – the attempt to secede, unlike the attempt to advance some irridentist claim, is never a *mere* move within the existing system of inter-state power rivalries. Secession depends on group sentiment and loyalty – not just on a disputed title to land or a doctrine of prescriptive right. In the final analysis, it is a form of mass politics organised from below rather than imposed from above through propaganda and the apparatus of the state. In this sense, it constitutes the nationalist challenge to the society of states taken to its logical conclusion and therefore in its purest form.

A tentative conclusion may be drawn from this observation: other things being equal, it seems likely that irridentist claims (except where they are supported by powerful secessionist sentiment) will be defeated if and when they are submitted to legal arbitration. The conclusion is tentative because international lawyers themselves will not lay down general principles in the absence of an authoritative judicial ruling on the matter; which in this case is lacking. The fact that the British, Spanish and Argentinian governments have all refused to seek the opinion of the International Court of Justice on the status of Gibraltar and of the Falklands/Malvinas islands suggests that they still have doubts as to which way the ruling would go. Such evidence as does exist suggests strongly that, were an irridentist claim to be submitted to the Court on the basis of historical title only and without reference to the wishes of the inhabitants of the disputed territory, it would be regarded as an anachronistic hangover from the period of prescriptive right.

This conclusion can be inferred as much from claims which have not been submitted to arbitration as from those which have. Although the British have not been prepared to submit their sovereignty over Gibraltar or the Falklands to arbitration one would expect Spain and Argentina (the irridentist states in these disputes) to have sought a judicial ruling if they were sure of the outcome; but both governments have consistently refused to do so.

The same conclusion can be drawn by reviewing the fate of the only competitor to the doctrine of state sovereignty to have survived into the contemporary world, namely the doctrine of suzerainty. Compare for example the case of Tibet[15] with that of Morocco. When the Chinese communists invaded Tibet and the Dalai Lama fled to India in 1951, neither the Indian nor the British government were prepared to support Tibetan claims to national self-determination, and to sponsor Tibet's membership of the United Nations. The reason was that although the British had established a *de facto* protectorate over Tibet, as part of their policy of securing their Indian Empire against Tsarist expansion, neither they, nor the successor Indian government, had ever challenged Chinese claims to suzerainty. Throughout Chinese history strong governments in Peking had exacted tribute from Lhasa and weak ones, by their neglect, allowed the country to assume an isolated independence. There is little doubt that an extremely important factor in their decision to acquiesce in Chinese occupation was that neither the Indian nor the British governments had the ability or inclination to intervene militarily on the side of the Tibetans. But the acknowledged weakness of their own legal position *vis-à-vis* Tibet undoubtedly reinforced their lack of political will.

Morocco's claims to territory beyond its own borders (originally to the whole of Mauritania, more recently to Western Sahara) also rests on a doctrine of prescriptive suzerainty rather than on an appeal to the principle of popular sovereignty, even though these claims have always been popular with the Moroccan population. Originally, the Moroccan sultanate was not a territorial state in the modern sense and the ruler's authority, which was religious as well as secular, extended as far as his armies could march in pursuit of tribute, an event which, as in the case of China's relations with Tibet, occurred only at irregular intervals. However, Moroccan claims have twice been tested in international organizations – first with regard to Mauritania and secondly, to the Western Sahara.

In 1960, Morocco was briefly able to secure the support of the Arab League for its Mauritanian claims, and with the help of the Soviet Union, to keep Mauritania out of the United Nations. By the autumn of 1961 this support had crumbled and although the dispute rumbled on for some time, King Hassan formally abandoned the claim in 1969 and the next year concluded a Treaty of Solidarity with the Mauritanian government.[16] In 1974, acting through the United Nations, Morocco again sought to establish the validity of a territorial claim, this time by requesting an Advisory Opinion from the World Court on the Western Sahara. The Court's judgement accepted that historically there were 'loyalties of allegiance' between Morocco and some tribes living in the territory, but also held that these could not be used to pre-empt or withhold the right of a local population to self-determination.[17]

If this conclusion holds, territorial irridentism may not constitute a permanent or standing threat to the international order. Claims to title of this kind belong to the same intellectual and diplomatic world as arguments about the legitimate ceding of territory to another state as part of a dynastic marriage settlement, or as in the case of Quebec, as a result of defeat in war. Secession, by contrast, does constitute a standing challenge to an international order based on the sovereign state. It does so because, on the one hand, it belongs to the modern 'rationalist' world in which the right to self-determination is held to be a fundamental human right, while, on the other, aggressive war, and therefore the possibility of acquiring title by conquest, is proscribed under the United Nations Charter. The only way out of this impasse is to resort to the conventional interpretation of national self-determination as reflected in the existing state order. This is so obviously a fiction that it must in turn constitute a provocative invitation to secessionist nationalists.

THE PRECONDITIONS FOR NATIONAL SUCCESS

The short, but largely accurate answer to the second question which I raised earlier – namely, under what circumstances is the nationalist challenge most likely to succeed – is that territorial revision is very rare and so presumably therefore are the circumstances which are conducive to it.

On one account there are in the world about 8,000 identifiably separate cultures; yet there are only 159 independent states.[18] Clearly the odds on a successful nationalist assault on the existing state order are very long. Why should this be so? The obvious answer is again straightforward. The three great waves of modern state creation – in Latin America in the nineteenth century, in Europe after 1919, and in Asia, Africa, the Caribbean and the Pacific after 1945 – have all been associated with the collapse of empires. There are no more empires to collapse and therefore very limited possibilities for further state creation by this route. I refer here, of course, to formal imperial structures, not the informal systems of economic and political influence such as those headed by the United States and the Soviet Union. These hegemonic systems no doubt limit, in varying degrees, the actual independence of their subordinate members, but since they do not obliterate their legal status, any nationalist revolt against the prevailing order, as in Hungary, Czechoslovakia and Poland on the one side, or in Cuba and more recently Central America on the other, is a revolt *within* the existing territorial dispensation not against it.

The conclusion is strengthened by the fact that, for different reasons, the two superpowers share the general bias within the society of states against territorial change. The United States is currently opposed to revolutionary change which is almost invariably viewed by Americans as a victory for communism, despite the justification of secession contained in the Declaration of Independence. The Soviet Union has always regarded support for the principle of national self-determination as a tactic to be pursued when it would advance the cause of the revolution rather than as an end in itself, despite the right of secession which is enshrined in the Soviet constitution. And, as the time approaches when non-Russians will outnumber Russians in the Soviet population, it is a fair guess that, even as a tactic, they are likely to be reluctant to support secessionists in case they reopen the national question within the Soviet Union itself. It is, therefore, not merely legal and political opinion within the state system which has attempted to freeze the territorial map; this outcome also corresponds to the interests and policies of the two major powers. Since secessionists must take on the state, they have little choice but to seek external assistance; and on the evidence advanced so far little hope of obtaining it.

It is not true to claim, however, that there has been no territorial change since 1945 other than that brought about by the withdrawal of

European imperial power; nor that secessionists have been totally unsuccessful in appealing for outside help, even from the super-powers. This is an area in which the dangers of false analogies are more than usually apparent – except in the underworld of gun-running, there is no international solidarity amongst secessionists and it is difficult therefore to apply the analysis of one case to that of another. Nonetheless the record suggests that there are three sets of circumstances under which the negative conclusion that secession is doomed to failure should be relaxed, or at least qualified.

Regional patronage

If the two superpowers have been reluctant to support secession, the strategic stalemate between them has on one occasion provided the opportunity for a regional power to come to the assistance of a nationalist movement. To show how restricted such opportunities are in practice one need only compare the pattern of external assistance to the Bengali struggle against West Pakistan, which led to the creation of the state of Bangladesh in 1971, with Somalia's unsuccessful efforts to solicit support for the struggle of the Ogaden Somali against Ethiopia. In the former case, American diplomatic support for Pakistan was cancelled out by Soviet support for India; and although the American sixth fleet manoeuvred in the Bay of Bengal, and the Indian Prime Minister, Mrs Gandhi, signed a friendship treaty with the Soviet Union before she took any independent action herself, India was able to intervene, and to inflict a humiliating defeat on the Pakistani forces, without seriously risking the escalation of the conflict. India, of course, had interests of its own in coming to the support of the East Pakistan Bengalis: the civil war was inflicting an intolerable and politically dangerous refugee burden on Bengal, notoriously one of India's most volatile states; at the same time the dismemberment of Pakistan would put India's hegemony in the sub-continent beyond question. For a year or so the new state was kept out of the United Nations, but by 1974 the *fait accompli* had been accepted and Bangladesh was recognised, even by Pakistan itself.[19]

By contrast, in the Horn of Africa, while the two superpowers were similarly in stalemate, there was no local power with sufficient interest in the conflict to defy the norms of international society. Successive Somali governments recognised that they could only secure their pan-Somali goals with external support. But neither the Soviet Union, with which Somalia was allied between 1969–1977, nor the United States after the Russians had been expelled from Mogadishu were willing to challenge Ethiopia's territorial integrity. To have done so would not only have risked a direct confrontation between the two superpowers, but would also have alienated the rest of Africa whose governments were determined to maintain the existing territorial settlement. It is not possible to say which of these two 'scenarios' is more typical of the contemporary international scene, but the fact that Bangladesh is the only completely new state created by secession since 1945 should perhaps provide a warning against generalisation from this single example.

Superpower competition

Although the American and Soviet governments have refused to commit themselves openly in support of nationalist movements whose aim is to secede from an existing state, their ideological rivalry has often led them to encourage ethnic separatism covertly and manipulatively. In such cases their motive is presumably to weaken the other side or secure a short-run tactical advantage in their own power political struggle. As we have already noted, Soviet support for the principle of national self-determination has always been primarily tactical, so it was a matter of little surprise that they supported the Eritrean struggle before the Ethiopian revolution and withdrew their support afterwards. Similarly, at the height of the Sino-Soviet dispute, which was also a period of close relations between China and Pakistan, the Soviet Union allegedly supported the Baluchi nationalists in their insurgency, but took care to stop well short of encouraging them to press their cause to the point of secession from Pakistan.[20]

The Americans have also frequently encouraged separatist movements as a way of obtaining leverage in their global diplomacy. One of the clearest examples is provided by the support which the Shah of Iran and the Americans together provided to the Kurdish rebellion in Iraq.

In 1975, a leaked United States Congressional intelligence report made it abundantly clear that an independent Kurdistan was not on the agenda. Instead the United States 'preferred ... that the insurgents simply continue a level of hostilities sufficient to sap the resources of our allies' [Iran] neighbouring country [Iraq]. This policy was not imparted to our clients [the Kurds] who were encouraged to continue fighting.'[21]

Although the issue is not one of separatism, it seems clear that American support for Jonas Savimbi's UNITA in Angola is similarly dictated by considerations of extraneous political expediency. In this case the motive appears to be American hostility to the MPLA government whose victory in the Angolan civil war depended on Soviet and Cuban assistance, and their desire to pressure the Angolan government into cooperating with the United States and South Africa to secure an international settlement of the Namibian dispute. Presumably, from the nationalist point of view, such unprincipled support is better than nothing, particularly as it allows them to continue the struggle. Since international politics are notoriously unpredictable, for some nationalists who have no illusions about the realist political game, accepting such help may in the end prove worthwhile. However, if the Kurds, whose peoples are divided between Iran, Iraq, Turkey and the Soviet Union, are taken as the model, this seems most unlikely.

Constitutional separation

We must finally consider the possibility of secessionist demands being peacefully accommodated, of states putting themselves into partial liquidation in much the same way as the European powers scuttled their African empires after 1960. This final qualification to the conclusion that the territorial map has been frozen into its present shape once and for all is the most conjectural of all.

If we discount the breakup of Malaysia, which was itself a creation of British decolonisation policy, and of such paper unions as the United Arab Republic (Egypt and Syria) and the Union of African states (Ghana, Guinea and Mali), none of which resulted in any real integration, the only relatively peaceful modern secessions were Norway from Sweden in 1905 and the Irish Free State from the United Kingdom in 1921. What if anything, of a general nature, can be said of the Swedish and British decisions to acquiesce in nationalist demands for constitutional separation?

Neither was unacrimonious, particularly the secession of Ireland which, given the turbulent history of British occupation, should arguably not be described as peaceful separation at all. On the other hand neither the British nor the Swedish governments were in the end prepared to preserve the unity of the state if that meant forcefully suppressing constitutional demands for separation and plunging their countries into civil war.

Behind their reluctance to preserve the unity of the state at all costs there were, it seems, two kinds of structural restraint. First, in all four countries there was an historical sense of identity, which preceded the nationalist era – and was generally acknowledged. In the case of

67

Sweden and Norway the union only dated from 1815 and was stated to be between two equal kingdoms.[22] In the case of Ireland, partly as a result of the machinations of the Protestant Ascendency, the English had never succeeded in co-opting the local Irish elite into the British system as they had done in Scotland and Wales.[23]

Secondly, at the time of these secessions, the contending parties were all led by liberal nationalists. It is true that the Republican issue introduced an additional complication to the British conflict with Ireland, but in the end, although it served to fuel the post-independence civil war in Ireland, its importance was symbolic rather than ideological in any deep political sense. The Norwegian and Irish nationalists shared the same political values and belief in the parliamentary system as the Swedes and the British; and this finally eroded their enthusiasm for maintaining unity by occupation.

Since the 1960s, the countries of the industrial west have witnessed something of an ethnic revival.[24] Where this neo-nationalist sentiment has been used as the basis of an armed insurgency against the state, and as a justification for urban terrorism (as with the Basque movement ETA or the Provisional IRA), it has been resisted with considerable determination and often ruthlessness. Where it has been used to mobilise a constituency within the framework of constitutional politics (as in Scotland and Wales in the 1960s and 1970s), there have generally been attempts by the state to accommodate regional demands for greater autonomy, always stopping well short of any discussion of independence. However, what would happen if having been granted a measure of autonomy, ethnic regions were to demand their right of self-determination and constitutional separation?

It looked for a time in the 1970s as though Quebec might provide a test case for the industrial countries on this question. The tide of Quebecois separatism seems to have ebbed, but if the demand for an independent Quebec was to re-emerge, and to be demonstratably supported by a substantial majority of the province's citizens, it seems unlikely that its separation would be resisted by force of arms, even though logically there would be no difference between the challenge posed by Quebec to the integrity of the Canadian state and that posed by Biafra to Nigeria or Bangladesh to Pakistan.

My conjecture is that while separation will undoubtedly be resisted, if the demand persists, it may be easier to accommodate in industrial societies than in other kinds of society where all opposition tends to be defined as treason. The plausibility of this conjecture rests on an assumption that a shared political culture, in which a belief in individual civil and political rights is deeply entrenched, will act ultimately as a constraint on the use of state power to suppress those rights. It is supported also by the vertical integration of the modern international system to which I referred at the end of chapter 2.

The integration of the modern world economy under the impact of liberal capitalism, has in many ways contributed to the modern nation-state, while the alleged inequity of the international division of labour has often fuelled nationalist reactions. At the same time, for those who are deeply involved in the world economy, it has undoubtedly raised the costs of dismembering the state. Modern enterprises generally prefer economic to political risk taking and are in a myriad of ways dependent on the state to provide them with a stable environment in which to operate. This tension between an economic nationalism, which is in part a response to economic integration, and the liberal world order is the subject of the next chapter.

5 ECONOMIC NATIONALISM AND THE LIBERAL WORLD ORDER

Many contemporary explanations of nationalism seek its roots in the transition from agricultural to industrial society viewing it as an ideology which arises either in reaction to the pattern of uneven development under the capitalist system, or to meet the need for some social 'cement', such as was allegedly provided in traditional society by organised relgion and/or folk custom.[1] I have avoided these arguments not because I consider the economic aspects of nationalism to be unimportant but because my purpose is to furnish an account of how nationalist theory and practice has been accommodated within the society of states, rather than to explain nationalism as a phenomenon.

It may be that historically the rise of nationalist doctrine followed closely on the break-up of traditional forms of society under the impact of industrialization. Undoubtedly, economic deprivation, real or imagined, has often ignited the flame of nationalist revolt. But the claims of nationalists are pressed in terms of national self-determination and success or failure is measured in terms of their ability to capture the state. What is claimed is freedom and independence for its own sake and not merely as a means of securing a more equitable distribution of income. Within the milieu created by nationalist thought it seems mostly unlikely that Palestinians would be prepared to sink their identity in a prosperous diaspora spread throughout an economically dynamic Arab world. It seems similarly unlikely that Black nationalism in South Africa can be bought off by coopting a satisfied but still disenfranchised African middle class into the system; or alternatively that Afrikaner nationalism will be forced to abandon its monopoly on political power by the logic of an expanding capitalist market. Yet these arguments have periodically been advanced by supporters of the South African government and their liberal critics respectively. Political power is undoubtedly valued because of the control over economic resources which it provides. But whether the formation of a particular national identity has economic

70

origins is a question which ultimately cannot be answered by empirical analysis. Nor would an answer necessarily tell us much about how nationalism affects the conduct of international relations.

No satisfactory account of the impact of nationalism on international relations, however, can ignore the economic dimension. It cannot be ignored, first because (regardless of the facts of the matter), the subjective experience of economic exploitation, and arguments about what is necessary to reduce it, have very often provided nationalist movements with their substantive ideology. Such ideological convictions can be specific, as for example in the Bengali conviction that they had been treated as an internal colony and exploited by West Pakistan, or general as in neo-Marxist arguments which are directed against Western neo-colonialism. I shall return to the relationship of these latter arguments to contemporary nationalism in chapter 8. The point to note here is that the belief that only the nation, organised not merely as a community in arms but as a territorial economy, can redress the wrongs of economic exploitation, mirrors the liberal view, that if only market forces are allowed to operate freely, the political cancer of nationalism can be cauterised at its source. Much of the contemporary debate about the international order turns out, on inspection, to be a debate between the supporters of a strong market and those of a strong, centralised, and collectivised nation-state.

A second reason for considering the economic aspects of nationalism is that, under the technological conditions of the modern world, command over scarce resources of either an economic or geopolitical kind is almost certainly a necessary precondition of success. We have seen in chapter 4 that it is not a sufficient condition, at the very least it is also necessary to mobilise external diplomatic support and to have an external patron who is willing to defy the norms of international good behaviour; but without something to offer the outside world, modern nationalists have great difficulty in being heard. The Biafran secession seemed credible because initially the leadership could make a case for a viable state based on oil. Without any similar bargaining chip the Southern Sudanese were virtually ignored by the outside world for more than a quarter of a century.

Third, and most importantly, we cannot ignore the economic dimension because the international economic system has been very largely shaped by nationalism or, more precisely, by a process of confrontation and compromise between the doctrines of economic liberalism and economic nationalism. The purpose of this chapter is to sketch how this confrontation came about, what it is about and the kind of compromise that it has produced.

71

Before turning to these rival doctrines, there is one point of definition which should be disposed of. It is sometimes argued that the term economic nationalism is a misnomer because the policies associated with the doctrine such as the pursuit of self-sufficiency, the protection of domestic production against foreign competition and a favourable trade balance, are as old as the state itself. From one point of view this criticism is valid: most of the economic policies which modern governments adopt to defend the nation are indeed similar to those adopted by pre-nationalist governments to increase the wealth and power of the sovereign. Particular groups of merchants or manufacturers may have benefited from these policies but mass sentiment was not involved, as it was once we enter the era of political nationalism.

From another point of view I believe the criticism to be misleading. It is not just linguistic carelessness that policies are now called nationalist which were once defended as supports of the mercantilist system: because the modern state formally rests on the doctrine of national self-determination (and even where it does not make this claim insists on its popular basis), economic policies which are adopted to defend and strengthen the state against foreign competition are adopted for explicitly nationalist reasons: for example, to protect industries which are considered vital for national security and prestige, or to maintain employment and social welfare policies.

Nationalism, therefore, sets limits to the emergence of a genuinely de-politicised world-wide market economy of the kind that many liberals have seen not only as the goal of economic policy but as a precondition for a harmonious international order. Nonetheless, the political victory of the nation-state at a time of unprecedented economic interdependence has had two paradoxical consequences. First, it has entrenched many mercantilist attitudes and policies and revived others. Secondly, it has created a general interest in a system of rules to govern international economic relations while constantly undermining the basis on which such a system could be erected.

To unravel these paradoxes we must look at the way in which the forces of economic liberalism (some of which were allied unwittingly to the nationalist expansion of the major powers) first challenged the pre-nationalist economic system, then established their own alternative orthodoxy (in which the links with nationalism were concealed by the doctrinal separation of politics and economics) and finally found themselves under siege as a result of the organisation of the state in both war and peace, on a national basis.

72

THE ECONOMIC FRAMEWORK OF THE EUROPEAN STATES-SYSTEM

Mercantilism

The period of European history which witnessed the centralisation of the state and the establishment of the jurisdictional monopoly of the sovereign, roughly between the sixteenth and eighteenth centuries, also saw the emergence of an economy whose boundaries coincided with those of the state.[2] The wealth of the state was regarded as a vital interest by sovereign princes for many reasons, but perhaps primarily as a war chest, a means of financing their wars and paying their often mercenary armies. The economic policies which they adopted for these purposes came to be called mercantilist.

Although there was never a single mercantilist doctrine, the economic policies of the period generally shared three overlapping features. First, economic policy was based on a view of wealth as finite and therefore, since wealth was necessary not merely for prosperity but also for power, on a pattern of international economic relations which was fiercely competitive.[3] Indeed, in modern terms the conception of international relations generally was zero-sum: in any exchange it was assumed that what one side gained the other lost. Thus, on one occasion, Colbert, Louis XIV's Finance Minister, described commerce as 'un combat perpetual en paix et en guerre entre les nations de L'Europe, à qui en emportera la meilleure partie'.[4]

Secondly, the competitive pursuit of power and the general pre-occupation with security which this entailed, led to a relentless pursuit of a favourable balance of trade, particularly whenever bullionism, the view that all wealth ultimately resided in precious metals, underlay state policy. In 1664 Colbert said: 'qu'il n'y a que l'abondance d'argent dans un Etat qui fasse la difference de sa grandeur et de sa puissance'.[5] Money can be secured by either plunder or exchange, but as Raymond Aron pointed out, in mercantilist thought there was no essential difference between the two methods.[6]

Thirdly, in varying degrees mercantilist policies accepted the regulation of the economic activities of the subjects of the realm as the norm. The general breaking down of earlier feudal systems of overlapping jurisdiction went hand in hand with the development of specific civil and eventually political rights, including property rights, which John Locke included in his list of inalienable human rights. The elaboration of these rights represents a crucial episode in the pre-history of modern capitalism, but for the purpose of the present argument the important fact is that they were guaranteed by the state. At the extreme, state regulation covered most areas of economic life, employment, production and above all trade. Since the farming of rights in any of these areas constituted a valuable source of revenue, it was sovereigns rather than private enterprises who first developed the practice of selling franchises.

The liberal challenge

During the eighteenth century, this framework of ideas and policies was attacked by the French physiocrats and the most prominent members of the Scottish Enlightenment, David Hume and Adam Smith. Their attack was mounted before the French Revolution, and thus before the rise of political nationalism, but two of its features have a critical bearing on the subsequent nationalist attack on the traditional system of states.

First, classical liberalism was part of a general rationalist attack on privilege and prejudice which culminated in the French and American Revolutions. Mercantilist policies, indeed the entire mercantile system as Adam Smith called it, was regarded as the economic bulwark of the *ancien régime*.[7] This system rested on privilege; accordingly mercantilist policies were regarded as shackles on the activities of free men. But intellectually, the rationalists held that mercantilism was also a false doctrine, held together by prejudice and superstition rather than the product of an enlightened and dispassionate examination of the evidence. Wealth, they believed, was not finite at all, let alone was it locked in precious metals; it was the creation of the productive enterprise of individuals. Under mercantilism, their energies had been constrained and controlled by the sovereign; it followed that the creation of wealth required people to be left free to pursue their own economic advantage.

Classical liberals did not believe that the unbridled competition to which the lifting of state controls inevitably leads, would in turn create a situation of social and political anarchy. This was because they also believed that there was a natural harmony of interests within civil society such that by pursuing his own interests the individual would also contribute to the public good. Adam Smith dubbed the mechanism, by which this harmony of interest manifested itself, the invisible hand.

The distinction between civil society and the state was crucial for this view of the world. It was not a classical liberal invention, but the major contribution of the liberal political economists to western

74

political thought was to develop its economic implications. Once they had done so it was possible to formulate a radically different conception of foreign policy than that of cut throat and bellicose competition which had obtained during the mercantilist period.

While mercantilists saw no essential distinction between war and commerce, liberal capitalists believed that commerce was essentially peaceful, the pursuit of rational men following their own interests. By contrast, they regarded war as an irrational anachronism, a way of settling conflicts of interest preferred by those who had for too long controlled the destiny of Europe and who frequently appeared to place passion and honour above sober analysis and calculation. Once it was clear that war had no role to play in increasing a country's wealth the way would be open to the creation of a cosmopolitan commercial society. They believed that this was the one legitimate kind of international society, which could arise from taking seriously the distinction between civil society and the state at the national level. When, after the American Revolution, Henry Adams went to seek an alliance with the French against the British, the original American draft treaty made a complete break with mercantilist thinking. The treaty proposed the immediate creation of a free trade regime, and the abolition of all distinctions between French and American citizens in each other's markets. This proposal dismayed the French who were looking for exclusive commercial advantages in return for protecting the infant republic against the British navy.[8]

Such a radical vision of a depoliticised international society did not survive for very long, even in the context of Franco-American relations. But it bequeathed to nationalists an ambiguous legacy which has always confused their attitudes towards the inter-state system. On the one hand, since many nineteenth-century nationalists were liberal constitutionalists, they tended to inherit the optimistic liberal view that trade was essentially a peaceful activity, and that economic internationalism would be a natural corollary of a world reorganised on the basis of popular sovereignty.[9] On the other hand, if the interests of the nation as a whole are paramount, rather than those of its individual members, there is bound to be a permanent tension between the implicit collectivism of nationalist thought and the rational individualism on which both political and economic liberalism are based.

The significance of this tension between collectivism and individualism may become clearer if we look at the second of its features which influenced the nationalist attack on the traditional system. This is the residual *étatism* and nationalism which, despite the explicit priority

75

accorded to individual interests, is nonetheless concealed within liberal theory.

Their advocacy of *laissez-faire* policies led the classical liberals to support a minimalist state. But it was no part of their argument to attack the state as such. On the contrary, by the time they launched their attack the state was so firmly entrenched that it was taken for granted, indeed regarded almost as part of the natural world. What frustrated the realisation of the harmony of interests, in their view, was not the state but the abuse of its necessary and legitimate (i.e. natural) functions. The liberal state was limited, but within its proper sphere, strong. Its first duty was, of course, to provide for the physical defence of the community – Adam Smith was in no doubt that if it came to a choice, defence was to be preferred over opulence.[10] Beyond that it also had to defend the institutions of civil society, including the market, by policing the framework of law and order without which these institutions could not operate, and by preventing the debasement of the currency.

Despite its rational individualism, and its dependence on a mechanical view of the social and political world, the concealed *étatism* of liberal theory was buttressed by an implicit nationalism. In contrast to Marx, Adam Smith regarded capitalist economic competition as an essentially cooperative, solidarist activity.[11] The underlying support for this view was the belief that the market would not be possible at all without the framework of law and order provided for civil society by the state. And since there were many civil societies and not just one, the historically specific community, like the state itself, was taken for granted. It was the community which, in the language of political theory, was deemed to have entered into a social contract. It was no accident surely that Adam Smith called his famous book *The Wealth of Nations*. Moreover, when David Ricardo developed the theory of comparative advantage, he assumed that there were cultural (i.e. national), as well as natural (i.e. resource) endowments which would determine the pattern of production and exchange.[12] In this sense nationalism as well as classical liberalism was part of the rationalist attack on the *ancien régime*.

The alliance between liberal rationalism and cultural nationalism could only be reconciled internationally under two conditions. The first would be if all states accepted the same internal constitutional discipline, made essentially the same distinction between state and society and accepted both that force should only be used in self-defence and that trade should be determined by commercial rather than political criteria. In other words, reconciliation would require that economic exchanges should be regarded as a private matter in which the state would not interfere.

The second possible reconciliation would be if one leading state was in a position to underwrite a liberal international economic order, so that even if all states did not accept the internal discipline of the liberal constitution, it would still be in their interests to accept the international regime. Failing that, they could be coerced by the leader into doing so. Since there has never been any serious prospect that international relations would be organised according to the eighteenth-century ideal of a cosmopolitan commercial society, it is via the second reconciliation (in which theory is ultimately subordinated to power political considerations), that liberalism has influenced international society, first under British and then under American leadership. By the same token the resulting order has always been vulnerable to a nationalist counter attack which represents the liberal order as a hypocritical veneer over what in reality is a system of imperial hegemony.

LIBERAL INTERNATIONAL SOCIETY

During the second half of the nineteenth century when British industrial and imperial hegemony was still secure, economic liberalism moved from its marginal position as a doctrine which aimed to subvert the traditional order at home and abroad, to become the ideological orthodoxy of the strongest power.[13] This achievement was to bring about a radical separation of politics and economics, or rather to dignify with the support of theory, a separation which earlier capitalists had pragmatically taken for granted whenever they could. As one economic historian has put it:

> The international capitalist ... has generally been, where business was concerned, a man without a Country, and the seventeenth century Amsterdammer though by no means a man without a city, was strikingly uninhibited by abstract considerations of patriotism or theories of economic nationalism.[14]

The formal elaboration of liberal political economy, however, had the paradoxical entailment that economic boundaries no longer enjoyed any intellectual or cognitive status, whereas physical boundaries continued to define the state in a political sense.

Ultimately this distinction was a fiction. Yet it would be wrong to underrate the radical impact of classical liberalism on both the theory of international relations and on how in practice they were organised.

77

Economic liberalism was a modern doctrine in a real sense: it made no essentialist assumptions about a natural hierarchy of power or about the rights of political groups to their own exclusive markets. On the contrary, the expansion and contraction of markets within the state and internationally was to depend solely on the interplay of supply and demand.

Eventually, as economic boundaries lost their political status, certain apparently anti-statist and anti-nationalist policies were derived from the liberal scheme. If markets were to be unregulated, the factors of production, capital and labour, had to be free to move across political frontiers at will.[15] And if individual consumers were to be free to buy in the cheapest and producers to sell in the dearest market there had also to be a system of multilateral rather than bilateral payments which in return required there to be a common medium of exchange – the function performed through most of this period by the gold standard.

The policy at the centre of liberal international society, however, was free trade. This was because it satisfied three major liberal beliefs: that it was a logical consequence of the system based on property rights, since free men had to be able to dispose of their own property as they saw fit; that it would produce the most efficient allocation of resources; and, that it was a vital support of a peaceful international order. In theory, given the principle of comparative advantage, any country which opened its markets to foreign competition would gain, even if the rest of the world remained protectionist, although this would not of course be conducive to mutual trust. In practice, the commercial order of liberal internationalism required from the beginning some way of reassuring countries that if they opened their markets to a neighbour, following a reciprocal exchange of concessions, they would not subsequently suffer as the result of a third country offering more advantageous terms. With the Cobden Chevalier Treaty of 1860 between France and Britain, a solution to this problem was found by basing commercial relations between states on the *most favoured nation* (MFN) principle.[16]

Until the First World War the liberal international order provided the framework of economic relations between the major powers. No doubt it owed more to the strength of the British economy – in most parts of the world sterling was as good as gold – and to the policing of world trade routes by the British navy, than to the abstract laws of classical political economy. Nevertheless, the period of classical liberalism saw the creation of the first ever interdependent world economy. It was the most powerful states, and above all Britain, which were most in favour of breaking down the barriers to international trade, just as earlier it had been the new commercial class in Britain whose interests demanded a competitive labour market and thus led them to press for the reform of the Poor Laws. The argument for free trade, in other words, was the logical continuation of their attack on government restraints that were imposed on them domestically. But for those who came late to the industrial race, the self-evident rationality of free trade was never so apparent. In their view economic liberalism was little more than a form of expansionist nationalism. The *Pax Britannica* thus led, economically as well as politically, to a more narrowly conceived nationalist reaction.

THE LIBERAL ECONOMY UNDER SIEGE

The nationalist challenge to the liberal ascendency was mounted first in the nineteenth century, by those who were opposed in principle to liberal cosmopolitanism and then, in the twentieth century, by those who reacted, either defensively or aggressively to the crisis in world capitalism during the inter-war period. In both periods principled and pragmatic, aggressive and defensive arguments were often combined. As with nationalist thought in other areas, the prototype of both these currents of argument was developed in Germany, although the arguments themselves had been deployed and developed in many parts of the world at different times. Both also adapted and extended various mercantilist policies and assumptions for specifically nationalist purposes.

Economic policy and national identity

The first of these adaptations sought to make economic policy an essential support of national identity. The nationalism which was a product of the German romantic movement was in some respects an early precursor of the 'nation-building' strategy adopted by many third world leaders in the 1950s and 1960s. Like them, the romantics were aware that the nation they were striving to conjure into being did not really yet exist. Its creation was also made more difficult by the penetration of liberal ideas in general and the liberal economic ideology of the strongest powers, Britain in particular.

Unlike many of their third world successors, who have constantly been seduced by the values inherited from the former imperial powers, the romantics felt relatively secure about the nature of the identity they wished to create. They opposed liberal cosmopolitanism

79

in principle – for them a man without a country was incomplete, somehow less than a man – not merely because like many later liberal nationalists they favoured infant industry protection. Their objection to cosmopolitanism, however, had some startling economic consequences: thus, for example, Adam Muller argued for a purely paper currency whose national identity could be guaranteed rather than one based on gold or silver which were in world-wide demand and consequently degenerate.[17]

This line of argument was extended by Johann Fichte whose *Closed Commercial State* (1800) adapted traditionalist mercantilist ideas to nationalist use. It also extended them by providing a blue-print for a complete collectivist society in which production, distribution and exchange would be planned as national activities. The need for foreign trade would be progressively reduced and eventually eliminated altogether, as the nation expanded to its 'natural frontiers'.[18] When this point had been reached it would be possible to contemplate an international situation without conflict, although it would hardly amount to an international order since there would be no need for international contacts of any kind.

The idea of 'natural' frontiers has always exercised an appeal to nationalists, for economic as well as for the irridentist reasons discussed in chapter 4. If the ideal of autarky or self-sufficiency is to be achieved without the population having to accept a reduction in its existing standard of living – the impact of autarky on future economic growth is not here the issue – this can only be achieved by domesticating the resources which were previously obtained by international trade. It is quite obvious that while some frontiers – for example mountain ranges, deserts, lakes, the sea surrounding islands and so on – may seem more plausible than others, particularly if they have persisted for a long time, none is natural: they are political and cultural, usually established by conquest and maintained by occupation. If, as Fichte proposed, nationalists aim at autarky, they will be driven ineluctably towards military expansion and a world view in which only the claims of certain economically and militarily powerful 'historic' nations need to be taken seriously. There is an essential similarity between the logic of Fichte's idealised argument and the policies that Hitler's economic minister, Dr Schacht, pursued in subordinating the economies of the Balkan countries to those of the Third Reich, even before Hitler embarked on his policy of military conquest.[19]

From one point of view irridentism and economic expansionism – to occupy a historical nation's idea of its 'natural' frontiers – might be thought of as opposites. Irridentism seeks the essence of national identity in the re-occupation of an ancestral homeland, ultimately a static conception; economic expansion seeks it in a dynamic conception of historical development in which a particular people's energy and enterprise give it a right to both the space and the resources which it needs to fulfil its destiny.

From another point of view, the practical difficulty faced by irridentists and economic expansionists is essentially the same. The one tries to re-establish the frontiers of a nation by reference to nature, the other by reference to a doctrine of manifest destiny and economic necessity. This difficulty consists of other people, members of other nationalities who live in the territories which have to be redeemed or conquered as the case may be. If the State, enclosed in its 'natural' frontiers, is regarded as an essential support of the nation's identity and its exclusive economic preserve, theoretically there are three alternatives, none of them attractive except to the most brutal realist.

The first is banishment: get rid of the people who don't possess the requisite national credentials. In economic terms, this presupposes that the pool of truly national labour is sufficiently large to exploit the resources of the national economy and to replace those jobs which *have* to be done to keep any modern society functioning, and which were previously occupied by those who have been driven away as a result of the occupation and/or redemption of the national patrimony.

This course of action also presupposes that the economic fortress which is thus created will be immune to retaliation. But what would happen if the displaced population became a burden to the country, to which it is driven? Clearly the feasibility of this option will depend on the numbers involved and the tolerance and absorptive capacity of the host country's population and economy. In the twentieth century, mass population movements have accompanied the attempt to redraw the political map along national lines with depressing frequency. But it remains difficult to think of a case of national self-sufficiency achieved primarily as the result of a policy of banishment.

The second possibility is genocide. Unfortunately it is not difficult to think of twentieth-century examples of this method of purifying the national stock. But although the most notorious example – the final solution of the 'Jewish problem' proposed by the Third Reich – was partly justified in terms of their alleged financial cosmopolitanism, the Jews were a scapegoat. Had that policy (alone amongst Hitler's projects) succeeded, it would not have had the effect of making the German economy independent of the rest of the world. To take one example: in 1939, German industry was still heavily dependent on

Sweden for imports of iron, steel and ball-bearings. Germany had neither conquered Sweden nor was it at war with that country.

Perhaps the only wholly successful case of genocide as a solution to a national, or at least an ethnic economic problem, is provided by an episode in British imperial history – the systematic extermination of the native population of Tasmania between 1800 and 1850 by British settlers. It may not have been official imperial policy, nor was the objective to close the state off from the outside world, but it was nevertheless a version of the manifest destiny argument pursued with a vengeance. The attempt was successful because it left no possibility of revenge. There were no native Tasmanians who in time, and with the benefit of western education and political concepts, could regroup, form a nationalist movement and set about reclaiming their ancestral homeland.

There have been other less completely successful attempts by 'historical' peoples from Europe to take over the lands, and therefore the means of subsistence, of the aboriginal and technologically inferior inhabitants of the countries in which they settled. The most famous, or infamous, of such cases is the conquest of the North American Indians whose identities were, in a very real sense, bound up with their system of economic organisation. Like the Amazonian Indians, whose long-term survival continues to be in doubt, the native North American population was decimated but not eliminated. From a political and economic point of view, the difference is small. Where these groups survived, they have done so very largely outside American civil society and the American economy; and because, tidied away in their reservations, they posed no democratic threat to the European majority.*

The third way in which economic policy can be used to support the

---

* In recent years there has been a growth of political consciousness and activity amongst North American Indians, particularly in Canada. An educated 'modern' leadership has emerged. Using the media to publicise their grievances and the courts to press their claims, they have demanded self-determination and even, on occasions, petitioned the United Nations on the grounds that their fundamental human rights have been denied. A similar process is beginning in Australia – even in Tasmania people claiming part aboriginal descent have sought a measure of restitution from the government. In these cases, the use of the idiom of self-determination is not employed to assert a right of secession but to reclaim lands which have been alienated. It is claimed that the loss of their lands is sometimes the result of a deliberate breach of the original treaties between European settlers and native peoples and sometimes the imposition of 'unequal' treaties in the first place. Political campaigns of this kind are only possible because, formally, the people involved have equal rights within a liberal constitution. The fate of indigenous peoples in many countries where discrimination is taken for granted, is even less fortunate.

national identity is by employing a system of helotry, that is, using the labour of a deliberately subordinated population, but denying it both the economic opportunities and the civil and political rights which are provided by the national state. The most spectacular modern case of this strategy is provided by the Republic of South Africa. With a contrariness which is typical of the country, it was often the early South African liberal nationalists who favoured a complete separation of the races, economically as well as politically, on the grounds that the antipathy between black and white was so deep that if they remained within a single system it would not be possible to develop a society based on liberal values.[20] By contrast the Founding Fathers of Afrikaner nationalism, those Boer farmers who embarked on the great trek to get away from the British, believed in a divinely sanctioned racial hierarchy which had originally justified their possession of slaves and continued to require an unambiguous master-servant relationship between the races.[21]

Given the development of South African industry by international, particularly British, capital on the basis of 'native' i.e. low cost, labour, there was never the remotest chance that the liberal project of racial autarky would succeed. Instead, after their capture of political power in 1948, the National Party developed the most comprehensive system of helotry in the modern world. Since the Afrikaners were critically dependent on both foreign capital and foreign markets, they generally supported the goals of the liberal international economic order abroad. But at home they used the patronage of state power to advance the economic interests of their own supporters against the more prosperous English-speaking community. A complex system of job reservation was also maintained, which seriously limited the economic opportunities open to blacks, and of urban influx control which denied them permanent rights of residence in white South Africa. Simultaneously, the government removed such few civil and political rights within the system that the majority black population had enjoyed before the National Party came to power.

Helotry is incompatible with most contemporary world views, but shortages of labour during times of rapid economic growth have often led western industrial countries to import workers temporarily from economically more backward countries. In some cases, Germany for example, these *Gastarbeiter* have enjoyed neither rights of permanent settlement, nor access on equal terms to the social and welfare services provided by the state for its own nationals. The existence of such helot enclaves, while potentially embarrassing to the governments of the countries concerned, is fairly easy to conceal because of their small size

83

relative to the overall national workforce, and because, to some extent and over time, the problem is self-correcting: when the demand for labour falls the guest workers can be sent home by the simple device of not renewing their contracts.

In the South African case the helots constitute the overwhelming majority of the population and there is effectively nowhere else for them to go in hard times. The government argues that the black population can exercise its political and civil rights in one of the 'independent homelands' from which they originally came. But the South African insistence that they are behaving no differently from other industrial countries has always seemed massively unconvincing to international opinion. No other country than South Africa itself has recognised the independence of the homelands. From all available evidence the policy of separate development has also failed to win over the majority of black South Africans. It can hardly be denied, however, that the National Party has deliberately and successfully used economic policy to buttress the position of whites in general and the national identity of Afrikaners in particular.

In nationalist thought, the ideal of autarky, of closing off the state economically, is rather like the ideal of free-trade, of a completely open and depoliticised market, in liberal thought. Where these ideals are entertained, we are likely to find a particular set of assumptions and a style of policy-making. In neither case has the ideal ever dictated all of the policies actually pursued by governments, but it has set the tone, collectivist in the one case, individualist in the other.

Under a system of modern helotry the autarkic impulse can be kept alive, even in a highly interdependent and dynamic world economy, by drawing a sharp distinction between the internal and the external economy of the state. Internally, the splitting of the labour market allows the state to extract a surplus from the helot population which can be used to support the identity and lifestyle of the nation in whose name it exercises authority. Externally, it allows them to achieve the same end by attracting foreign capital. Capital is attracted by the political 'stability' which is, in turn, ensured by the coercive apparatus the state has to maintain to keep the helots in line; and by the prospect of high returns on capital invested which is ensured by the artificially depressed price of labour.[22] Both internally and externally the terms of involvement in the economy are set by one national group only. In this sense the deliberate use of economic policy to support national identity is almost inevitably collectivist.

Economic defence

The second nationalist challenge to liberal international society was mounted against the background of the recurrent crises to which the capitalist economy was prone. This challenge arose within the liberal argument itself.

It is possible to endorse many liberal economic beliefs, for example, the belief in the superiority of market pricing over other ways of taking decisions about the distribution of income, or in the importance of appeals to individual self-interest in promoting enterprise and growth, or in the desirability of engaging in international trade, and to reject completely any mystical, romantic or essentialist conception of national identity. Further, it is possible to endorse all these liberal beliefs and still finish up believing that the state must have an ultimate responsibility to defend the national economy. Indeed, as we shall see in the next chapter, this belief has been repeatedly strengthened in the course of the twentieth century as national governments have contemplated the social and political costs of their involvement in a volatile world economy from which there is no easy escape. Here, it is sufficient to note the origins and general structure of policies of national economic defence.

In accounting for their origin we need only recall that the classical liberal distinction between the open economy and the closed state was a powerful fiction, but a fiction nonetheless. If economic boundaries had really counted for nothing, as liberal theory suggested, then there would have been no distinction between domestic and foreign trade. Since states and nations were regarded almost as part of the natural order, in practice distinctions were always maintained between domestic and international trade and between exports and imports. From the beginning, therefore, the concept of a national economy was embedded within the concept of an open market. It is difficult to see how it could have been otherwise even at the time; and with the advent of popular sovereignty and mass politics, it is impossible. National income accounting which all modern governments regard as an essential basis for rational policy-making would be impossible without the aid of such distinctions.

Structurally, the liberal policy of national economic defence has two aspects. The first derives from the state's responsibility to protect the community in the event of war; the second from the need, which was perceived early on in the debate, to create conditions in which latecomers to the international market could gain entry.

As regards the first aspect we have already seen that the early

85

liberals argued for a state which was simultaneously minimalist and strong. Its primary political task was defence, which dictated that self-sufficiency as a means of warfare was to be preferred even if the state did not enjoy a comparative advantage in the manufacture of armaments. Its primary economic task was to maintain stable prices which were regarded as necessary to promote confidence in the market order. To this was added, at least in the case of some classical economists, a duty to protect agriculture again for reasons of security rather than efficiency.

The second aspect of liberal economic defence policy involved using tariffs as a temporary protective expedient. Although Alexander Hamilton had developed what later became known as the infant industry argument to justify protecting American manufacturers against British competition, and as a way of creating a local market for the products of American agriculture, it was Friedrich List who developed the argument for protection most systematically in his *National System of Political Economy*, published in 1840.[23]

List was a nationalist and politically an opponent of the English school of liberal political economy; but intellectually he accepted much of their argument. He was a leading advocate of dismantling the complicated system of tariffs and customs duties which the German states maintained against one another and of creating a customs union, the *Zollverein* for Germany as a whole. This union was to be strongly protected against foreign competition particularly from England. He thus provided the intellectual defence of nationalist protection in the interests of wealth creation in a competitive market system; in other words, he advocated government manipulation of the national market both as a means of integrating a powerful national community, and to enable that community to catch up economically with its stronger competitors. Once they had done so, the system of protection could be replaced by a system of universal free trade, which would then no longer constitute a threat to any properly constructed national economy. In this sense his argument provided the model for much twentieth-century developmental nationalism.[24] The third world, it might be said, once began on the Rhine.

In time, the implicit nationalist assumptions of liberal theory, which in the case of Germany, List had made explicit, were everywhere accepted in whole or in part. Since the end of the First World War, the pressures of interdependence have reinforced the general drift to official intervention in the economy in the interests of national protection, particularly during times of world recession. Two other developments have contributed to this process: the necessity for a command economy to fight modern wars, and the emergence of a purposive, rather than merely a regulative, state. A purposive state is one which regards it as its duty to secure for the population not merely their rights to physical security and property but also to welfare.

Before turning to these developments in the next chapter it is worth noting the weakest point in this cosmopolitan liberal scheme. It was also the first part to be abandoned in favour of a national order of economic defence. Logically, an open market order requires the free movement of labour across international frontiers. By the turn of the century, however, immigration control had become the norm. Many ardent nationalists believe nationality is a natural attribute, defining human beings in the same way as their physical characteristics. If, for most liberals, nationality has never been regarded in quite so unambiguous a light as this, bureaucratic rationality has nonetheless set practical limits to the idea of a world of completely mobile and free individuals. It is true that the market is both a very seductive and a very powerful force: by the mid-1980s a thousand people a day were said to be crossing the Rio Grande illegally, and no industrial country outside the communist bloc was immune from the problem of illegal immigration. The fact that even in the most liberal societies, immigration is regarded as a privilege not a right, suggests that there are compelling practical arguments in favour of the national state.

6 THE NEW ECONOMIC NATIONALISM

At the height of the great depression in 1934, Maynard Keynes argued that governments should, so far as possible, pursue policies of national self-sufficiency.[1] Keynes was not a romantic nationalist – indeed, his instincts were unashamedly those of a cosmopolitan intellectual – but he was convinced that, in the absence of effective international machinery, national governments had to take unilateral action to overcome the problem of mass unemployment and to lay to rest the spectre of communist revolution to which it had given rise throughout the capitalist world. He also believed that, if governments intervened in the economy to raise the level of effective demand, they *could* resolve the problem.

By 1945, most western politicians and intellectuals, including Keynes himself, were convinced that any revival of economic nationalism would threaten the new international order to which they were committed. The proliferation of tariff wars, competitive devaluations and other 'beggar-your-neighbour' policies during the 1930s, was widely seen as having contributed to the economic failure of the industrial countries and, politically, to the rise of fascism and the drift to war. It is by no means certain that this belief was well founded; but, as in other areas of international relations, this hardly matters, it was the perception that counted. In any event, the central objective of the economic peacemaking on which the western allies embarked in 1942, was to construct a system of economic cooperation between states which would provide insurance against such a revival.[2]

From the start their efforts were complicated by the fact that the logic of economic nationalism, unlike the logic of earlier mercantilist doctrines, pointed in two directions, only one of which was perceived to be malign. As we saw in chapter 5, nationalist doctrine always carries within it a potential for xenophobic intolerance, but at the same time it accords with the bureaucratic rationality of a state based on the principle of popular sovereignty. It was only the first of these ingredients that the peacemakers attempted to purge; the second they tried desperately to accommodate.

This postwar attempt to split the benign from the malignant aspects of economic nationalism was only partially successful. By the mid-1980s, even this partial success had been substantially undermined. The attack came from three directions: from the failure of the industrial democracies to adjust the international economic system, so as to accommodate the expansion of the state's responsibilities to provide for social and economic as well as physical security for its citizens; from a revival of protectionism in the industrial world in the face of economic decline, rapid technological innovation, and the increasingly effective challenge posed to their economies by a group of successful third world countries; and from the failure of the reconstructed international order to accommodate the collective aspirations and nationalism of the third world. The first two of these challenges will be discussed in the present chapter and the third in chapter 8. In order to see how they have combined to attack the liberal international economic order, we must first consider in more detail the nature of the compromise between economic liberalism and nationalism on which the postwar economic system was constructed.

THE POSTWAR SYSTEM

United States war aims

Following the collapse of the fixed exchange rate system in 1971, an academic debate has developed over the issue of hegemony.[3] The question is whether a liberal international order, in which the rules of the market are enforced over the particular national interests of individual countries, requires the leadership of a hegemonic power. This debate need not concern us here except in one respect: the system that was established after 1945 would not have taken the form that it did, and would possibly not have been set up at all, without American leadership.

In 1945, not only was the United States the one major industrial power whose economy had survived the war intact, but it was the one non-communist country whose leaders had a clear ideological conception of the kind of international society they wished to construct. The Americans had not won the war single-handed, nor could they make the peace just as they pleased; but the war could not have been won nor the peace made without a major commitment of American resources.

89

However, it is more important for the present argument to note that the liberal ideology on which the system was based, was designed to further some specifically American national objectives and to protect some specifically American interests. The assumed identity of interests between the United States and the system at large, emerged very early after the end of the war. Economic liberalism was already well-established domestically in the United States as the 'natural' ideology of the American people. But historically, the American industrial economy had developed behind high protective barriers against the outside world. It was therefore the extension of the open market philosophy to the international sphere which allowed American governments to argue plausibly for the identity of their own interests with those of the general international order. Two examples will serve to illustrate this general point.

The first concerns the anti-colonial theme in American foreign policy. From the late 1940s anti-communism was to dominate American views of the outside world. Immediately after the war, however, it arguably took second place to the government's determination to prevent the re-establishment of imperial power, and British imperial power in particular. Throughout the 1930s and 1940s the Americans had supported the Indian National Congress in its campaign to force the British out of India. During the war, Roosevelt had visited North Africa and encouraged the Moroccan king to secure an end to the French protectorate at the earliest possible date. He did so, not merely because the Americans supported the independence of colonies for its own sake, but because the opening up of the Moroccan market on a non-discriminatory basis would create opportunities for economic cooperation with the United States. Indeed, in all the major documents of the Second World War, the Americans insisted on including amongst the allied war aims a commitment to end preferential trading.

The second example of how specifically American national interests were reconciled with the commitment to an international liberal order, concerns the choice of an exchange rate system. There was general agreement on two propositions. The first was that it was undesirable to attempt a simple return to the gold standard (particularly for countries with limited gold reserves and/or a commitment to preserve full-employment policies). The second was that there could nonetheless be no return to the monetary free for all of the 1930s, the unpredictability of which, it was believed, had helped to prolong the economic depression and poison the political atmosphere. Beyond this there was significant disagreement about the kind of system to adopt.

Keynes had originally proposed a scheme which would have had the effect of giving all states an equal stake in the maintenance of monetary order. At the same time, it was designed to give them maximum individual freedom to pursue their own national economic and welfare policies. Very roughly, it involved treating balance of payments surpluses and deficits as morally neutral or equivalent, by providing a symmetrical set of incentives to debtors to export and creditors to import. Outstanding international transactions were to be settled in a new international currency – bancor. This currency would be issued by an International Clearing Union which would have the authority to grant generous overdraft facilities to debtors and with which the creditor nation would be required to bank their surpluses.

The obvious analogy is with the way a domestic bank offers credit to its customers at a price which normally increases with the size of the overdraft. In Keynes's Clearing Union proposal this analogy operated for those in debt only: while they would have no difficulty in negotiating lines of credit, the larger the deficit became and the longer it persisted, the more expensive such borrowing would become. The break with orthodox financial principles lay with the treatment of surplus countries: the larger their reserve holdings became, and the longer they persisted, the more expensive such holdings would become – a system of escalating bank charges providing the incentive for these countries to open up their markets.

Although this ingenious scheme was designed with the international interest in mind, one objection to it was that it favoured Britain, and other countries which were heavily dependent on world trade, at the expense of the United States and countries whose economies depended primarily on the home market. This was because the formula that was advanced to fix the initial entitlement to the new currency (and to credit limits) gave more attention to trade dependence than to existing reserve holdings or absolute size of GNP.

In any event, the proposal was too revolutionary to have any chance of securing Congressional support in the United States. In 1945, not only was the United States the major creditor nation (with two-thirds of the world's gold supply held in Fort Knox), but they were determined to choose a system which would limit the long-run danger of other countries devaluing against the dollar, thereby shutting the Americans out of their own market.[4] The dollar exchange standard, in which the parities of all the major currencies were fixed in relation to the dollar, which was itself pegged to gold at $35 an ounce, was partly chosen to secure this specifically American national interest.

The institutional framework

Both these examples illustrate the ambiguous relationship that has always existed between liberalism and nationalism. It is the essence of liberal political theory that universal rules should be adopted which apply equally to all without fear or favour, that is, without reference to specific historical contexts or interests. Yet as soon as an attempt is made to operationalise liberal theory it becomes unavoidable that such reference be made. This is as true in the international as it is in the domestic political arena. In practice, in the postwar context, it meant that, despite the attempt to deny national interests any official status in the new system, they inevitably re-entered by the back door.

It would be wrong to conclude that this ambiguity applies only to the ideology of the strongest power with the capability of determining the overall shape of the system. It may be the case that liberalism was the 'natural' ideology of the American nation after 1945, as it had been of Britain in the mid-nineteenth century, but in order to establish a liberal international order it was necessary to make concessions to the national principle which applied to other states in equal measure. Indeed, while many writers have described the post-war order as an American imperium, it is important to grasp the way in which it differed from all previous imperial systems.

Unlike these empires, the United States had to legitimate the liberal international order which it established as the vehicle for its indirect control. The nature of the new *Pax Americana* was such that international institutions had to be established to preside over the new economic order. In turn, this meant that the Americans had to make major concessions to nationalist sentiment, or at least they had to recognise the priority accorded by governments to national sovereignty, in order to ensure their consent. By contrast, during the period of the *Pax Britannica*, the British had certainly required legitimation of their overseas dominions in the eyes of the British people, or at least in terms of British constitutional practice – the Colonial Secretary was accountable to parliament like any other member of the government – but the maintenance of the British Empire had not depended on the formal consent of the colonised people themselves.

The underlying objectives of the two Bretton-Woods institutions – the International Bank for Reconstruction and Development (the World Bank), and the International Monetary Fund (IMF) – were

92

impeccably liberal. By supporting a revival of private capital markets, and underpinning the convertibility of major currencies, they were intended to encourage the freest possible movement of goods and services across international frontiers. This objective would also be promoted by the elimination of physical controls on trade and the reduction of tariffs negotiated within the General Agreement on Tariffs and Trade (GATT). Although the intention was to remove national sovereignty over exchange rates, in practice the IMF could do no more than curtail it, as governments insisted on retaining the ultimate responsibility in their own hands. Within the GATT, the commitment to trade liberalisation on the basis of non-discrimination and the most favoured nation principle was purchased at the price of a series of specific exceptions which were written into the agreement.

None of these exceptions was deliberately or consciously framed with reference to nationalist doctrines, but in different ways they all reflected the extent to which nationalist assumptions had become entrenched within modern political thinking. Thus Article XII allowed the return to protection in the event of a chronic balance of payments crisis. This was the nearest the GATT came to a specific admission that the political commitment to full employment should in the final analysis have priority over the economic principle of comparative advantage. Similarly, Article XVIII allowed for protection of infant industries for purposes of national economic development, and Article XIX as a defence against unforeseen and serious injury to domestic producers, again to allow governments time to take the necessary, and necessarily interventionist, measures to adjust the national economy. In terms of liberal theory the most significant exception was Article XXI, which allowed governments to withdraw market concessions unilaterally for reasons of national security. Before discussing the implications of these exceptions for the 'new' economic nationalism, we should consider briefly the final exception to the principle of non-discriminatory trade on the basis of the MFN principle.

At first sight, consideration of Article XXIV may seem inappropriate in a discussion of nationalism, since it is addressed ostensibly not to the priority of the national interest but to the desirability of regional integration. Closer scrutiny will reveal that it is the most telling of all the exceptions. The GATT allowed for only one breach in the 'no new preference rule'. Preferential trade would be permitted if it led eventually to the creation of a Customs Union or Free Trade Area. The theoretical justification for this departure from neo-classical ortho-doxy, was the trade creating effect that would be likely to follow for the world economy as a whole as a result of the merging of national markets, and the consequent opportunities that this would create for manufacturing industry to exploit economies of scale.[5]

For the present argument, it is not so much the theoretical justification of the Customs Union exception which is of interest (particularly as its practical significance has always been highly dubious) as the implicit political assumption on which it was based. Presumably, this was that if states agreed to merge their markets, they would be taking a first, cautious but peaceful step towards an ultimate change in their political identity. Given the voluntarist character of liberal theory in general, and the theory of self-determination in particular, this possibility has to be allowed for; moreover, its theoretical appeal is considerably enhanced when we recall the almost insurmountable difficulties which arise if the problem of political nationalism is addressed head on.

While it envisages the possibility of transcending the national principle, the Customs Union exception also testifies to its strength. The process which culminated in the establishment of the EEC in 1957 was greatly accelerated by the refusal of the French Assembly to contemplate the creation of a European Defence Force in 1954 let alone a more comprehensive federal union between France and Germany. The subsequent history of the EEC, in which progress towards the merging of national economies, and national economic policies, always proceeds at the pace of the most reluctant member and, through the mechanism of trade-offs between distinct interests, also testifies to the continuing vitality of the national idea. And what applies to western Europe applies even more strongly to other parts of the non-communist world.

Virtually all the attempts to establish Customs Unions and Free Trade Areas in the third world have aborted for a combination of two reasons.[6] First, in the absence of supra-national institutions with the power and authority to redistribute income within the new entity, the removal of obstacles to the free movement of goods and services across national frontiers has the perceived effect of providing disproportionate benefits to the economically strongest state. This, not surprisingly, also has the effect of hardening rather than softening national sentiments and antipathies. Secondly, when governments have newly acquired sovereignty and/or are primarily concerned with their political and economic vulnerability, they generally show a marked reluctance to create such institutions. Even when they do so, they display an equally marked tendency to restrict their competence and ignore their authority. The evidence from integration schemes seems conclusive: economic interdependence within the world market has undoubtedly shaped the context of contemporary international relations, and in numerous ways created both opportunities for and restraints on government policies; but, nowhere has it supplanted the nation-state or established a new focus for popular loyalties.

National security and economic order

The state itself, and the legitimating idea that it should ideally be a national state, has a stubborn resistance to withering away. Nonetheless it is symptomatic of the modification that the international environment has brought about in modern nationalism, that of all the exceptions to the GATT, Article XXI (which was designed to allow states to discharge their essential security functions) has hardly been used at all.[7] To understand its neglect, we need to consider both the intellectual background to the GATT and the world in which it operates. The most plausible explanation is that Article XXI represents a carry over from an earlier international society, rather than a reflection of the political world we have actually inhabited since 1945.

The concept of security has never fitted easily into liberal international thought. On the one hand, as we have seen, the state has the prime duty of defending its own citizens. Hence, in the event of war and for its duration, the privileged independence of the market from political interference is suspended. Hence too, the provision that is made for such a contingency in the GATT, since in theory peacetime trading partners may find themselves at any time on opposite sides in an armed conflict. On the other hand, the underlying liberal assumption is that the development of the international division of labour, and of the interdependent world economy to which it will give rise, will maximise general welfare and thus raise the costs of conflict. On this view, any attempt to advance the national interest by force will appear increasingly irrational. In other words, the maintenance of a market order, and the commitment by states to its progressive liberalisation, is itself the best form of security policy.

Until the Second World War, this tension in liberal theory was masked by a combination of the prevailing technological and ideological conditions. Although the possibility of war had to be entertained, the state's duty to defend the nation did not include participation in permanent standing alliances. Other considerations apart, it was not necessary to have such alliances in order to put an army in the field equipped with the latest weaponry. Nor was there then an ideological fracture in the inter-state system which would have justified the creation of a standing military alliance or, for that matter, the elaboration of a multilateral framework of commercial rules and a system of management covering economic relations between states at different levels of economic and social development. Indeed, the international system could not have been constructed in this way without interference with the spontaneous growth of markets and the spread of commercial cosmopolitanism, to which liberals attached such importance.

During the inter-war period the major fracture in international society was within the capitalist world. Like generals, economists have a tendency to fight the last war. When it came to peacemaking at the end of the Second World War their thinking was conditioned by the negative experience of competitive economic nationalism during the 1930s rather than by the new configuration that emerged with the onset of the cold war.

Since the danger was identified with the economic nationalism of capitalist states, the peacemakers were prepared to depart from the pure doctrine of *laissez-faire*, which required no institutional infrastructure, in order to preserve its essence, the maintenance of a stable international economic order. The institutional system which they created (i.e. the IMF, IBRD and GATT) was originally conceived as a universal framework for the world economy. Its creation depended on political agreement but its purpose was to depoliticise so far as possible its day to day functioning. In retrospect it is not clear how it was ever envisaged that two sets of national economies (those organised on market principles and those based on state ownership and central planning), were to coexist under a single set of liberal rules. In any event, the issue was never put to the test. Stalin would have nothing to do with it. In his view the new institutions were no more than the economic infrastructure of the Western Alliance. Although East–West economic relations gradually expanded, and acted, during the 1970s, as a crucial support of *détente*, they have never been effectively removed from the political arena of national and ideological rivalry.

If the creation of the system of liberal multilateralism was intended to protect the 'free world' against the economic danger of a self-destructive atavism, the establishment of NATO in 1949 was designed to furnish states, which could no longer hope to defend their independence single-handed, with a permanent military shield. Such a shield was necessary because, while only the two superpowers could now involve the world in a general war, they confronted one another first in Europe and then in Asia rather than directly. It was also necessary because the advent of nuclear weapons created the need for war avoidance or deterrent strategies, i.e. those which removed, so far as possible, the elements of uncertainty and unpredictability, from the balance of power.

So long as this system holds, Article XXI of the GATT is unlikely to be used, precisely because the major threat to the peace among the industrial powers does not emanate from within the capitalist system itself but from the confrontation between the capitalist and communist worlds. And because this confrontation is structural rather than contingent, the commercial rules which states are permitted to suspend for reasons of national security have never applied in East–West relations.[8]

The period between the early 1950s and the early 1970s was one of unprecedented prosperity and growth in the western world. Consequently, in relations amongst themselves, the governments of the western powers had no reason to return to the world of competitive economic nationalism. It was only towards the end of this period, that it became clear that the cold war and the confrontation of the two great standing alliances which sustain it, had broken the nexus between economic liberalism and the wider framework of international security. The widely shared assumption, that economic growth was causally related to the process of liberalisation, concealed a deeply paradoxical consequence of the postwar order. In effect, by insulating their economic order from their security system, the western powers had not eliminated the phenomenon of economic nationalism as they had thought, but had made the world safe for it.

How could this be? In 1945 it had seemed plausible to believe that the beggar-your-neighbour policies of the inter-war period had not only helped to prolong the great depression but had contributed to the drift to war. By contrast, the period since 1974 has been marked by repeated protestations by western leaders of the dangers of the protectionist revival and their determination to reverse it. But it has also been marked by their repeated failure to match their policies to their words. The unavoidable conclusion seems to be that, in the final analysis, they do not take the danger seriously.

There has been a significant return to protectionism in most industrial countries. However, while arguments across the Atlantic about the protection of the steel industry, or European and North American complaints about Japanese penetration of their automobile or audio-visual equipment markets, undoubtedly put a strain on alliance relationships, in the end they have to be patched up. The risks of pursuing trade wars to their logical conclusion are just too high: in a world of nuclear confrontation no one seriously believes that such disputes could possibly be the direct, or event indirect, cause of war between the western industrial nations.

ECONOMIC NATIONALISM AND SOCIAL SECURITY

If the combination of superpower confrontation and nuclear technology has reduced the political risk associated with economic nationalism, the new responsibilities of the state have significantly raised the social and political costs of internationalist over nationalist policies. There seems little doubt that the immediate if not the root cause of the 'new' economic nationalism is to be found in this relationship between falling political risks and escalating social costs. We have already noted that after 1945 a deliberate attempt was made to differentiate between the malign and benign forms of economic nationalism, and to accommodate the latter within the liberal order. The justification for this accommodation ultimately stems not from the logic of the market economy but from the logic of mass society and popular sovereignty. To the extent that modern wars have a tendency to become total wars (i.e. wars requiring conscription, the mobilisation of the civilian population as well as the military, and the institution of a command economy) governments must be prepared in an emergency to demand that the people should make the ultimate sacrifice. But since modern governments, at least theoretically, *belong* to the people, at the end of the war it also becomes increasingly difficult for them to treat labour merely as a commodity.

By 1945, the new logic had become inescapable. In the first British postwar election the people rejected Winston Churchill, their wartime leader, largely because they feared that the Conservative Party had not accepted it. In Italy the commitment to full employment was even written into the new constitution of the reconstructed republic. Indeed, after 1945, the mixed economy and welfare state emerged as a dominant political form throughout the industrial west, although significantly at a much slower pace in the United States than elsewhere. The break with the past, however, was not quite so dramatic as this account may suggest.

The problem of maintaining a strict separation between civil society and the state, and consequently of confining the state's responsibility for security to military defence, was not new. In successive editions of his *Principles of Political Economy*, J. S. Mill had expanded his chapter on the 'Limits of laissez-faire' as he realised that only the state could finance a system of universal education and provide public goods such as adequate roads, drainage and other public health facilities.[9] Nor is the separation between the old concept of physical security and the new one of social security as complete as the original liberal theory might suggest: if the state must be able to call on *all* the citizenry in the event of war, then public health, nutritional levels and so on, automatically become matters of national rather than merely private concern.[10] And as the technology of modern warfare becomes more sophisticated, so the level of mass education also becomes a public matter – the new cannon as much as the new industries need literate fodder. However, in one respect there was a major new departure.

The decision to regard the level of employment, and hence the overall performance of the economy, amongst the list of public goods was a postwar innovation with far-reachng implications. The chief of these was to qualify the modern industrial state's commitment to the liberal economic order. So long as the liberalisation of the economy was associated with high growth rates, increases in productivity and a perceived improvement in the general standard of living, the economic nationalism of industrial societies remained latent. Once the association ceased to seem obvious to all but those trained in neo-classical economics, it quickly manifested itself.

The costs of interdependence

Of the many political and economic developments which contributed to this switch in public perceptions, three have a particular bearing on the relationship of the new economic nationalism to the arrangements of international society. The first is an increased awareness amongst industrial governments of the costs as well as benefits of economic interdependence. Originally the liberal state had not worried about costs because economic relations fell within the private domain and the burden of adjustment fell, like an act of God, on the unfortunate population which had to adjust by its own efforts.

Few postwar liberal states could afford to take such a relaxed attitude to the problem of adjustment: by instituting state pension and unemployment pay schemes, they had acquired a direct interest in reducing the cost to the public revenue which would arise as a result of high levels of unemployment and a loss of international competitiveness. They had also acquired an interest in maintaining a high level of economic activity which alone could generate the income required to cover constantly growing levels of public expenditure.[11]

Demography raised the cost of the new liberal state still further: falling death rates throughout the industrial world meant that, just as

99

the state had accepted a responsibility to provide social as well as physical security, it found itself responsible for the welfare of an increasing proportion of the population who were too old to form part of the national work force.

Awareness of the costs of interdependence does not mean that any of the western industrial states can contemplate contracting out of the international division of labour. As President de Gaulle discovered during the 1960s, even closing a national market to private foreign investment may prove more costly than putting up with the loss of control that participation entails. These costs – and they are political as much as economic – have to be measured in terms of lost employment opportunities and the risk of a permanent loss of competitiveness as a result of lagging behind in the acquisition of new technology. What an awareness of economic vulnerability does mean, is that with every down turn in the economy, western governments are constantly on the lookout for ways of cushioning the burden of adjustment for their populations and so reducing its cost to themselves.

The search for damage limitation policies has the inevitable consequence of making governments sensitive to sectional pressures for protection. By calling on the doctrine of comparative advantage, it is relatively easy to demonstrate that protection is against the national interest. The hero of the classical liberal system has always been the consumer whose interest obviously lies in being able to buy in the cheapest market. On this view the argument for protection becomes positively anti-national, particularly if free trade is regarded as a prerequisite for the creation of wealth.

But if we change the angle of vision from the consumer demanding his rights to a free market to the citizen with his growing list of demands on the state (for the provision of education, health, public utilities, old age pensions, and unemployment pay), it is no longer so obvious that a government which gives in to protectionist pressure from a particular industry or trade union, is thereby acting against the national interest. If a major section of the labour force is suddenly thrown out of work as the result of foreign competition, not only will there be a high financial cost to the state but there may also be high social and political costs as disaffection spills over into other sectors of the economy, possibly giving rise to a more virulent, xenophobic and less controllable form of nationalism.

This problem was recognised in the postwar system. An attempt was made to deal with it by allowing governments to engage in temporary protection during periods of structural adjustment. But there are dangers in such an approach. In the most notorious case, namely the series of multilateral arrangements through which the international trade in textiles has been regulated since the early 1960s, what started as a temporary expedient, to deal with the social problems of a declining industry, appears to have become a permanent feature of the international economic order. The reason for such breaches in the liberal trade order is not difficult to understand: once public money has been directed to particular industries, for example, to allow them to modernise by introducing labour-saving equipment, implicitly a political case has been made for regarding that industry as a strategic national asset. It then becomes difficult for any government to withdraw its support.

Sweden even invoked its traditional policy of neutrality as a justification for its adopting a more restrictive attitude to imported textiles from the third world than the other industrial countries. The Swedish argument was that it faced two particular problems which distinguished it from other industrial nations. The small size of the Swedish population was held to make it more difficult for its industry to exploit economies of scale than in countries where the domestic market is larger. Second, the Swedish authorities argued that, being without allies during a war, the country must have contingency plans based on the concept of self-sufficiency. They therefore aimed to maintain a 'minimum viable production' in the textile sector by a combination of industrial subsidies and protectionist policies.[12]

The interest of the Swedish case for the present argument does not lie in the success of this policy – in fact Sweden has been even less successful than other industrial countries in preventing the penetration of its market – but in the fact that the policy of neutrality allowed them to make the strategic argument, on the grounds that the state has a duty to give priority to national defence. Other industrial countries find the pressure for protection equally irresistible, and judging by their behaviour also regard the textile sector as strategic (in an economic rather than a military sense). But since their political as well as their economic policies bind them into a system of multilateral interdependence they cannot so easily reconcile protection with their public commitment to the liberal trade order.

The truth of the matter is that *all* the industrial democracies face essentially the same dilemma: how to reconcile a dependence on the world market, and therefore a need for open market trading rules, with the electoral imperatives to manage the economy and provide an adequate level of services. Protection may not be an ideal solution to this dilemma. Nor is it a particularly efficient solution; it is not, for example, preventing third world producers from progressively increasing their share of the world textile market.[13] But precisely for this latter reason, it may be a relatively harmless response to the policy dilemma which the governments of the industrial nations face. And in any event in relation to sectors of the economy which employ a significant proportion of the labour force, and/or have important linkages elsewhere in the economy, it may be politically unavoidable.

The failure of incomes policy

The second postwar development which undermined the liberal order was paradoxically the weakening of national cohesion in societies which had been freed from immediate physical threat and were enjoying a prolonged period of material affluence. We have already noted that within the tradition of liberal political economy there had always been an implicit assumption of national solidarity. This assumption was not merely taken over but reinforced in the Keynesian challenge to neo-classical orthodoxy.

As a pragmatist, Keynes accepted the territorial nation state and addressed his theory to the solution of its practical policy problems.[14] When he wrote his major work, moreover, there was so much under-utilised capacity in the industrial world that he was able to propose that the government should raise the level of effective demand by deficit spending, without worrying too much about sectoral and inter-industry rivalries. The nation was united in adversity almost as clearly as if it had been facing a military invasion. His policy proposals were aimed at achieving full employment at the national level. This was true for both his proposals for national self-sufficiency during the 1930s, and then after the war, for the creation of sufficient international credit to make the retreat behind national borders unnecessary.

It was no accident, then, that when finally Keynesian economics established itself as the new orthodoxy, its success depended on the maintenance of high growth rates: this was the only way that the soli-darist assumptions would not have to be put to the test. If the dangers of xenophobic collectivism are to be avoided and the liberal benefits of a tolerant society and an open market are to be enjoyed, the government must be able to distribute, by direct and indirect means, a suffi-cient proportion of the national product to give all groups a stake in the *status quo*. Once the governments of the industrial countries had to combat a combination of rising inflation and falling productivity (rather than stimulating demand, as a way of stimulating produc-tivity), the vulnerability of the solidarist assumption to sectional attacks was exposed.

Most of the industrial countries responded to this challenge by attempting to achieve a tripartite agreement between private employers, trade unions and the state itself. The state, in its capacity as a major employer in its own right and as a mediator between the other two parties, sought agreement on the planned growth of incomes and prices. In other words, governments attempted to build a principle of restraint into the competitive market order. Experience with incomes policies has varied depending on the different institutional and economic histories of the states concerned – broadly they have been more successful in Austria, Germany and Scandinavia, less in Britain and France – but they have seldom been an unqualified success.[15] The essential reason is the inherent tension which exists between the twin bases on which such policies rest, the appeal to group interest and national solidarity.

Historically, societies have accepted very wide disparities in incomes over very long periods of time; but once these have been questioned – and given the egalitarian basis of modern nationalist thought such questioning is all but inevitable – the only logical (i.e. non-arbitrary) alternatives are a standard wage regardless of the nature of the work done, and fixing the price of work, like that of any other commodity, in a free market. Notoriously, neither of these two methods corresponds to how incomes are in fact distributed in the industrial world. Consequently, once an attempt is made to institute an incomes policy the government has little alternative but to ask all groups to accept the existing pattern of differentials 'in the national interest', and to accept equal restraint in future wage bargaining. Under this formula, the worst off have to accept a disproportionate share of the burden. Almost invariably they attempt to make a case for special treatment, provoking in turn an equally determined effort by more favoured groups to maintain the existing pattern. Once the policy has broken down under this combined attack, governments find it increasingly difficult to resist pressures for national protection. It is as though in advanced industrial societies, prosperity depends on international competitiveness, which in turn depends on a sense of national discipline and a willingness to accept restraint. Where these qualities neither arise spontaneously nor can be organised by government propaganda, as during the early stages of a war, modern governments have almost no alternative but to act in support of industry, both through the provision of subsidies and at the border.

The problem of raw materials

The final way in which the industrial states' preoccupation with social as distinct from military security has undermined the commitment to internationalist economic policies is through their determination to maintain reliable sources of raw materials. Their development of national energy and raw material policies is in part a reaction to the challenge from the third world which is the subject of the next two chapters, but it also stems from the two developments discussed above, namely the new awareness of the high social and political costs of interdependence and the failure of the state to induce a self-sustaining mechanism of national discipline and restraint.

A major American objective in proposing the new economic order was to contribute to the demise of European imperialism.[16] The economic dispensation of the old imperial order, however, was not seriously disturbed by decolonisation. The industrial world as a whole continued to import many of its raw materials from the former colonial territories. Little attention was given to the prospect that supplies, mainly but by no means only, of oil, might one day be interrupted for political reasons, or that the producing countries might be able to extract an economic rent from the industrial world as the result of scarcity. Moreover, since for obvious reasons of self-interest most of these commodities entered the industrial countries duty free, they were outside the purview of GATT, which concentrated on the abolition of quantitive restrictions to trade and the reduction of industrial tariffs. To a large extent, indeed, the rapid growth of the industrial world economy and its increasing integration depended on a steady supply of cheap energy and raw materials.

It was not surprising, therefore, that the sudden quadrupling of the price of oil in 1973/4 had a cathartic impact on the world economy. Apart from sharpening the north–south confrontation, it compounded the domestic problems of the industrial countries in two ways. The first was to expose the fragility of the assumed national consensus which underlay their demand management policies. The sudden rise in oil prices did not cause the great inflation of the 1970s but it greatly accelerated it. It led immediately to determined efforts by trade unions to negotiate higher wage settlements so that their members would not suffer a real decline in living standards as a result of the higher manufacturing costs. The consequence was to push the inflation rate still higher in a seemingly endless spiral. And because some trade unions occupied a more strategic position in the economy than others, the spiral of cost-push inflation put intolerable pressure on the spirit of national restraint on which the industrial governments had pinned their hopes.

Secondly, the demonstration by the oil producers that they could dictate the price of a strategic commodity, and the fear that the lesson

104

might be learned by third world producers of other commodities, persuaded western governments to look inwards, or to establish special ties with countries with which they enjoyed close political relations rather than relying on the traditional north-south division of labour.

Not all industrial countries were equally dependent on imported raw material and their response to the new situation varied accordingly.[17] Japan whose dependence was most acute, and whose spectacular economic recovery after 1945 owed much to the American Alliance, was the most alarmed. Suddenly, the *Pax Americana* on which the Japanese had relied, was shown to be flawed: if the United States could not prevent the Arab oil producers from discriminating against countries of whose foreign entanglements and policies they disapproved, could it be relied on to prevent the interdiction of shipping on the high seas? The Japanese response to this new fear was to establish close bilateral relations in South East Asia and Australasia by tying investment in new mining and other enterprises to long-term supply contracts.[18] Other countries such as Britain and Norway found that, in the energy field at least, the high oil prices that had been fixed by the OPEC countries as a means of extracting rent from the west, made it economic for them to exploit their own off-shore reserves. The paradoxical consequence was to make these countries unofficial supporters of the concept of formally managed energy markets, which had been developed by OPEC, initially in opposition to western interests. They could no longer afford to see the price of oil fall to levels which would threaten their own national investments.

More generally the industrial countries became weary of political instability in many parts of the third world which they no longer controlled. As a result new investment in the extractive industries was increasingly diverted to the exploration and exploitation of the raw material resources of the west itself, particularly in North America and Australia. The modern nation-state is in large measure a management structure; and while good management requires flexibility, it also requires predictability. Without reasonable confidence about future trends, it is difficult for any government to discharge existing obligations, let alone accept new ones.

This need for control is the major and largely inevitable result of the western preoccupation with social security and welfare. During the 1970s, third world countries pressed, unsuccessfully, for schemes which would tie the prices of their raw material exports to those of their manufactured imports from the west.[19] They argued, with considerable justice, that as a result of wage settlements in the industrial countries, the benefits of any increase in raw material prices was likely to be immediately wiped out in higher import costs. From the perspective of western governments, however, it was the unpredictability of raw material prices which threatened their efforts to contain inflation, and therefore the consensus which was necessary for economic management at the national level.

THE NEW INDUSTRIAL PROTECTIONISM

Although the redefinition of the state's responsibility to provide security (i.e. its widening to include the concept of social security in addition to its traditional obligation to provide military defence) provides the underlying rationale of the new economic nationalism, it has other sources which reveal the residual force of traditional nationalist thought. Economic liberalism is a fair weather doctrine. But even in fair weather, when the climate of expansion is likely to generate a relaxed and optimistic attitude to shifts in the international division of labour, most governments are unwilling to contemplate unconditional surrender to the principle of comparative advantage. In times of recession and/or rapid technological change, they are even more resistant to allowing market forces alone to dictate national destinies.

In the final analysis, it is the state's traditional concern with defence and with the provision of a framework of law and order which provides the key to understanding this resistance rather than its relatively new concern with welfare, although even here defence should not be interpreted in exclusively military terms. Some light may be shed on the residual economic nationalism of the industrial state if we consider the case of agriculture, the one area of the national economy, apart from military production, which even committed liberals have often been prepared to protect.

Agricultural protection

The actual reasons for agricultural protection – and in the contemporary world it is all but universal – vary widely. They range from the organised political power of farmers (whether yesterday's peasants in France or Italy or land-owners in Britain) through the deal between France and Germany which made the EEC's Common Agricultural Policy the political cornerstone of West European integration, to the problem of equalising the terms of trade between town and country which sooner or later has faced all industrial countries. The original

106

case for agricultural protection, however, was defensive: it was no good providing society with a military shield against foreign attack if, in an emergency, the population could be starved into submission through the mounting of an effective blockade. Although modern military technology destroys the credibility of this scenario for most industrial countries, none are prepared to contemplate the total destruction of the agricultural interest. And for those, like Sweden, which cling to the concept of military independence, agricultural self-sufficiency is still a basic ingredient of their strategy of economy defence.

In addition to the tariff, western governments have used a variety of other means of protecting the national market such as subsidies to farmers to enable them to match world market prices, levies imposed at the border which allow domestic producers to determine the internal market price, and quantitative restrictions. Even if there had been a general willingness to liberalise agriculture, the variety of protective mechanisms, and the different ways in which their use influences the politics of the countries concerned, would have made the exercise far more complicated than in the manufacturing sector where dependence on tariff protection created in effect a common currency – since the protective impact of a tariff could be measured – in terms of which mutual concessions could be negotiated.

Non-tariff barriers

The use of non-tariff barriers (NTBs) has never been confined to the agricultural sector, even though during the period of GATT liberalisation, roughly between 1947 and 1970, concentration on tariff negotiations obscured their impact on trade in manufactures.[20] There are many kinds of NTBs in use, ranging from customs valuation procedures to the application of national safety and health standards to imports. However, it is the practice of discriminating in favour of nationals in government procurement policy, which best illustrates the continuing power of national over international criteria in governmental decision-making. As with agriculture, the original and still underlying rationale of this practice concerned military defence.

When the state first entered the market place, it was generally to arm itself. The internationalisation of the arms trade has now reached a very advanced stage so that not only do all the major producers in the industrial world depend on export markets, but in many areas the United States and the Soviet Union have developed an absolute advantage, a fact which gives them enormous coercive influence amongst their subordinate allies. Nevertheless, military procurement continues to be an area where few would argue that decisions should be based merely on commercial criteria without regard to the wider national interest. Governments, in other words, have little choice but to exercise their judgement in balancing between considerations of cost-effectiveness and vulnerability.

Government procurement is not confined to military production only. The state has now become an important market for a wide variety of industries which are in a position to meet the requirements of modern government. Since military and civilian systems often use the same technology – computers for example – and since the research and development costs of high technology industries are likely to be beyond the means of any but the world's leaders, a national subsidy becomes essential if a country is to retain any kind of capability in one of the new 'sunrise' industries.[21] And once government money has been committed to an industry which is in a position to service the state, it becomes politically embarrassing to place government contracts with other suppliers. The fact that so many of the world's leaders are American and have risen to their current eminence on the back of defence-related government programmes – the American space industry is a prime example – inevitably reinforces the argument elsewhere for national industrial policies in high technology fields.[22]

The logic of industrial nationalism

Western liberals have sometimes argued as though nationalism was a passing phenomenon which in time would give way to a purely 'rational' organisation of society from which all appeals to metaphysical principles or mythical identities would have been expunged. Although they employ a different vocabulary, their essential views in this respect are not very different from those of orthodox Marxists who have always regarded nationalism as false consciousness. The argument of the last two chapters has suggested a contrary conclusion. In chapter 5 we saw how the nineteenth-century liberal economic order built on the achievements of the mercantilist period, and, more importantly, carried over from it several key political assumptions which were explicitly statist and implicitly nationalist. The argument of the present chapter has been that the new economic order constructed after 1945 similarly made explicit concessions to the national principle, and had embedded in it the seeds of a new round of protectionism. As the plant itself began to flower in the 1970s it became clear that a combination of moral and structural conditions was encouraging its propagation. Together these conditions may be said to constitute the logic of contemporary economic nationalism. If the argument is accepted, there is no reason to believe that either the dilemmas of national policy in an integrated world economy, or the appeal of nationalist arguments in support of state policy, constitute merely a passing phase in the process of economic and political development. It may be useful, therefore, to summarise this logic before turning to the phenomenon of third world nationalism.

The conditions which combine to forge the logic of the contemporary national state occur in two dimensions, one relatively static, the other highly dynamic. On the one hand, as a bureaucratic structure, the welfare state is necessarily an exclusive association, which under pressure is likely to justify its actions, ideologically, in nationalist terms – for on what other basis can they be justified? Ultimately, the defence of rights must be based on a capacity to exclude. On this view, indeed, the justification for the state, with its traditional monopoly of legitimate force, is that it enjoys a comparative advantage in the provision of this service.

This argument is normally advanced in support of the proposition that the proper functioning of the economy depends on the legal defence of property rights; but it applies with equal if not greater force to the defence of welfare rights. This is because once the state moves away from merely providing physical security and defending property there is no 'natural' cut-off point; positive entitlements can be extended indefinitely so that each time an extension occurs the cost rises and so does the political salience of deciding who can and who cannot claim the entitlement. Foreign passport holders are generally those who can be excluded most easily.

On the other hand the international context within which the state must discharge its traditional and its new obligations is dynamic, characterised by mutual economic penetration and interdependence and increasingly rapid technological innovation. In order to discharge its obligations, therefore, the state has no alternative but to adjust and compete. It was in response to this imperative that, during the 1980s, the governments of the United States and Britain launched a major assault on public expenditure. The British, in particular, made parallel efforts to return previously nationalised industries and public utilities to the private sector. Even where radical governments of the right attempted to 'roll-back' the state, what they achieved could more accurately be described as a 'stand-still'. The list of public goods did not grow, and, at the margin, some positive entitlements may have been withdrawn. But the enormous costs of maintaining the infrastructure of a modern industrial state were sufficient to ensure that, despite the rhetoric, such tactical retreats could not be turned into a strategic withdrawal.[23]

The liberal counter-attack on industrial nationalism has not yet run its course. However, it is already clear that structural constraints put massive pressure on the original liberal conception of society within which economic adjustment occurs without direct political intervention. Those same constraints also reinforce the national conception, within which the claims of citizens automatically take precedence over those of foreigners. Once it is accepted that there are no *inherently* strategic industries (i.e. those which can claim state support as a matter of necessity and right without reference to opportunity costs), the stage is set for a policy debate which can ultimately only be conducted in terms of the national interest.

The most obvious candidates for 'national' status will be the old and the new industries. In other words they will be the industries which have traditionally employed a high proportion of the workforce and whose precipitate decline would be likely to have alarming social and political as well as purely economic consequences. Or they will be those whose development is either too costly, and or/too risky, to occur spontaneously, but which may be judged necessary if the state is to continue to 'pay its way' in an open and increasingly competitive world market. The balance between the government and the market, and between adjusting to competition from abroad and taking the initiative, will no doubt continue to be struck by different governments at different points and at different times; but the preoccupation of western governments everywhere with industrial policy suggests that there is no available escape from the national framework of decision-making.

7 POST-COLONIAL NATIONALISM

In chapter 6 it was argued that the liberal world order has been substantially eroded by a powerful nationalist logic embedded in the organisations and values of western industrial societies. The purpose of the final two chapters is to examine the parallel failure of the reconstructed world order to accommodate the developmental nationalism of third world countries. In this chapter the intellectual and political foundations of post-colonial nationalism are examined; in chapter 8 the collective third world campaign to reform the international economic order.

In these chapters, the claim is *not*, as some authors have argued, that an essentially coherent and viable western system has been undermined by attempts to accommodate states and societies whose value systems are radically different to those of the West.[1] Perhaps Asian and African societies have found some western ideas indigestible, but the concept of the sovereign state is not one of them. On the contrary it is the most successful western export to the rest of the world. Rather, the claim is that the experience of third world countries in international relations provides further evidence of the underlying weakness of (and contradictions in) the liberal scheme of international cooperation.

Admittedly, for the student of international society, third world nationalism poses an unavoidable problem of evaluation. In the west, nationalism is very often considered to be a curse, whereas in the south it is thought of as a blessing. The explanation of this difference in perception can only be historical: in the one case nationalism is associated with war, destruction and irrational intolerance; in the other with progress, the transcendence of parochial loyalties and development. But regardless of such contrasts, in both west and south it is equally subversive of any wider international order.

The same conclusion emerges if we compare the typical preoccupations and political styles of industrial and third world governments. The industrial world is largely composed of well-established nation-states, whose political leaders generally eschew the more bombastic forms of nationalist rhetoric and ideology. This does not mean that western societies have somehow evolved beyond nationalism. However desirable, such an evolution is impossible so long as politicians attempt to manipulate (or appropriate to their own favoured policies), the mass public opinion on which they ultimately rely.[2] Such efforts inevitably limit how far they can pursue international policies (or commit themselves to schemes for international cooperation) when these run counter to perceived national interests. In other words, in all industrial societies, nationalism is a powerful constraining or mobilising force; but it is generally invisible, embedded in the social fabric and institutional practices of the state.

Throughout much of the third world, states are nation-states only in name.[3] In other words there is very often only the most tenuous fit between their systems of state authority and the sentimental and political loyalties of the mass of the people. The leaders of these countries almost invariably defend their policies in explicitly nationalist language, and ostensibly direct much of their energy to 'nation-building' projects and policies. (The purpose of 'nation-building' is precisely to transfer loyalties from peripheral areas and traditional authorities to the centre.) They therefore look to the international order for material and ideological support towards this objective. In these states nationalism is not embedded, and it is certainly not concealed; it is aspirational and problematic, sometimes capable of mobilising a mass movement, sometimes only touching the lives and experiences of a small westernised elite. However, since the objective is to create a mass public sentiment in favour of the state, nationalism also sets limits to the commitment of third world states to international cooperation. It is thus nationalism itself, not the stage of development of particular societies, which creates the international problem.

THE POLITICAL AND INTELLECTUAL BACKGROUND

In broad outline it is not difficult to account for the general character of third world nationalism and the points at which it confronts the prevailing international order. Its character is heavily coloured by the circumstances surrounding the transfer of power. The majority of Asian and African states are new in the sense that, until comparatively recently, they were ruled directly by one or other of the European powers. Many of these states are also new in the sense that their political geography was a creation of the colonial powers. This holds also for the previous generation of new states in Latin America which were creations of Spanish and Portuguese rule. Indeed, it also holds for the original new state, the United States of America, and for Canada. In their case, however, the nature of settlement and the source of colonialism allowed them to build national societies within a liberal constitutional framework. As we saw in chapter 3 the same historical legacy creates a somewhat more schizophrenic attitude amongst third world leaders. They owe their political prominence to the success of the anti-colonial revolt against the west, but in an obvious sense they are both heirs to, and beneficiaries of, the European imperial order. Inevitably both the conflictual and collaborationist aspects of this imperial legacy shape the nation and state-building policies of third world governments as much as do their attitudes to the principle of national self-determination.

The fact that, from the start, third world nationalism was anti-imperialist and anti-western, has led many third world leaders to seek an alternative ideological scheme to the liberal capitalism which they mostly inherited at independence. At the same time because so many Asian and African states are new polities, and even where this is not the case have been heavily penetrated by western education and values, there are very few genuinely indigenous political traditions on which they can draw. The idea of cultural authenticity is as appealing to many third world nationalists as it once was to the European romantics. But its doctrinal content remains as elusive now as it was then. Moreover, doctrinal content is more necessary now than it was in the nineteenth century. Modern nationalists need to do more than plead for the inalienable right to self-determination of a disenfranchised cultural group; typically they need also a programme for social and economic transformation. The reason is simply that they live within a world which is not only far more interdependent than was the case in the nineteenth century, but where their own central political concerns have shifted from constitutional to economic issues. More precisely a largely middle-class preoccupation with personal liberty has given way to a populist equation of independence and affluence.

In circumstances where third world leaders had necessarily to rely on ideological as well as manufactured imports, it is not surprising that many of them were attracted to Marxism. From their standpoint, Marxism (or rather Marxism–Leninism) had a double advantage. First, although in Asia and Africa it remained an exotic import, it had the advantage of being a dissident movement within the western tradition. As such, it met the essential criterion for third world nationalism in being strongly anti-imperialist. It was also anti-capitalist which for some leaders at least was an added bonus.[4]

Secondly, Marxism–Leninism also included a strong element of economic prescription. Once he had seized power, Lenin developed a non-capitalist strategy for rapid industrialisation. This strategy combined a monopoly of the means of production in the hands of the government with a concentration on heavy industry. Its purpose was to lay the foundations of an independent, and largely self-sufficient, economy. At independence, very few third world governments, even had they been so disposed, were in a position to adopt the Soviet model in its entirety. But there is no doubt that many were attracted by a philosophy which was anti-imperialist, anti-capitalist, advocated government control of the economy and promised quick results.

But if Marxism was attractive to many third world nationalists, the majority of them only flirted with the doctrine. They were heavily constrained from embarking on a Soviet-style development strategy by internal social and economic exchange and dependence. The attraction of Marxist doctrine was, in most cases, fairly superficial. This was partly because the imperial powers had made determined efforts to limit the exposure of Asian and African elites to Marxist writings, and more particularly Soviet influence, and partly because the nationalists themselves were, in any case, only attracted to those parts of the theory which were compatible with the primacy of the nation-state.

Marx's own views on nationalism were profoundly ambivalent. His basic position was that the proletariat had no fatherland and that nationalist doctrine was a form of bourgeois false consciousness. For tactical purposes he sometimes relaxed this position in specific struggles for national self-determination – broadly he supported or repudiated nationalist movements depending on his reading of whether success would advance or retard the cause of proletarian revolution.[5]

At first sight Lenin seemed to have put the Soviet state squarely on the side of the right of all peoples to national self-determination (there is even a right of secession in the Soviet constitution). But Soviet practice has always subordinated this right to the interests of the revolution and socialism whenever they were in conflict. However, probably more important for an understanding of post-colonial nationalism than a close reading of Marxist theory or Soviet history, of which many third world leaders were ignorant, was the fact that their own political education had been acquired in a non-Marxist and often anti-Marxist environment. Many of them had achieved power as the result of a long process of negotiation and relatively non-violent confrontation with the colonial power. At independence, they were in no mood to substitute one form of subordination for another, a consideration which largely explains the appeal of non-alignment. Even when they employed the Marxist political vocabulary (and endorsed the historicist faith in final victory over the forces of reaction which is central to the Marxist position) they invariably insisted that their Marxism came second to their nationalism.[6]

Not all third world governments were tainted with collaboration. But even for those which had fought their way to power, the practical constraints on pursuing a Soviet-style development policy were overwhelming. Apart from China, no third world country was in a position to contemplate rapid development on the basis of self-sufficiency. Nor was the assistance available from the Soviet Union. In the early post-war period Stalin refused to have anything to do with the first generation of Asian leaders, denouncing them as stooges of the imperialist powers.[7] Although he began to soften his position at the end of his life, the Soviet Union has not been prepared to underwrite the economic development of any third world country, with the spectacular exceptions of Cuba and Vietnam (and the still contested case of Afghanistan). Consequently, while third world nationalists have often borrowed eclectically from Marxist theory to buttress their anti-western credentials, and have used a neo-Marxist analysis of their economic plight for instrumental purposes (i.e. to purchase Soviet diplomatic support for their objectives and/or to buy off domestic criticism), they have tended to look to the western powers for assistance in overcoming the problems that lie beyond their own capabilities.

NATIONALISM AND DECOLONISATION

The third world has confronted the international order on two major issues. The first, which is discussed below, concerns decolonisation, its justification and extent. The second, which is the subject of chapter 8, concerns the collective efforts of third world governments to influence the international system to their own advantage. In different ways both issues also raise the question of whether the legitimacy crisis in many post-colonial countries was a consequence of their involvement in the international system, or could be overcome with international support.

The international context

It was American liberalism rather than Soviet Marxism which set the stage on which the drama of anti-colonial nationalism was enacted,

115

and its greatest triumphs recorded. As we have seen, in 1945 the Americans regarded the British Empire as a major obstacle to their plans for an open, non-discriminatory world order.[8] In particular they elevated the abolition of preferential trading to the forefront of their war aims. In the early postwar years, before the cold war changed their priorities, they also lent their support at the United Nations to third world states in their campaign to speed up the process of decolonisation, and to extend the principle of international account-ability from the trusteeship territories to the remaining colonial possession of the European powers. It is true that the American addiction to capitalism was viewed with suspicion by some post-colonial leaders (for example Nehru) but, for most, the political weight of the United States and its leverage over the Europeans, was suffi-cient compensation.

It was during this period also that it became clear that in the post-colonial world, economic development would be the central nationalist objective. Indeed, third world nationalism was, in most countries, almost synonymous with the drive for economic develop-ment. This simply reflected the widespread perception (correct in some instances, merely convenient in others) that its absence was a direct consequence of colonial exploitation and neglect. In 1956, India embarked on its ambitious second five-year plan which aimed to build up the country's industrial base and to make it self-sufficient in agricultural production. As the European empires were rapidly dis-mantled, each new successor state followed suit, proclaiming its determination to overcome the ravages of the past.

Although European governments understandably resented the charge of neglect (arguing that they were responsible for building up the modern sectors of the colonial economies), from the nationalist viewpoint, the concentration on development was an appropriate response to a fundamental problem. Once alien rule had been dis-lodged, the new rulers faced the oldest question in politics: by what right do you rule? In the heady atmosphere of the anti-colonial struggle, the organisation of a movement for self-government had been sufficient legitimation; once the goal had been achieved some-thing more was required to underpin the exercise of power.

The answer which the majority of third world governments gave to this question was that they alone were in a position to complete the process of decolonisation by presiding over a programme of rapid economic development and social modernisation. 'Seek ye first the political kingdom and all else will be added unto it.' Kwame Nkru-mah's famous prophecy provided the general formula. With independence the successor governments had achieved the political kingdom; what they now had to deliver was the 'all else'.

From the start there were exceptions, a few countries where political boundaries were congruent with traditional authority. In pre-revolutionary Iran or Ethiopia, in Nepal, Morocco, Swaziland and Lesotho, Saudi Arabia and the Gulf Emirates, economic development was no doubt an important concern of governments. They too had to exist in an increasingly interdependent world in which their subject populations were constantly, if precariously, exposed to outside influences. But in these countries, economic and social transformation was not initially their central political imperative. In nation-building terms they possessed a usable past. In other countries, and particularly those of South East Asia, the immediate issue both before and after decolonisation, was the recovery of autonomy by political communities of great antiquity. The political future and allegiance of Vietnam, Cambodia, Laos and Thailand was certainly a contested question, but not the identity of the people concerned.

There were also always some, mostly small, countries whose numbers have sadly swollen in recent years, where power seemed to be regarded merely as its own reward. In this 'non-ideological opportunist fringe' to use Ernest Gellner's phrase, little or no attention was paid to either the imperatives of nation-building or the legitimation of government.[9] But for the majority of new states economic development was not just a technical question; it was the one strategy available to governments which was at once undeniably modern (and therefore legitimate by virtue of this fact) and seemed to offer a means of detaching loyalties from clan, tribe and region and transferring them to the new state-nation. This was generally the case even where one of the world religions still exercised a strong hold over the affections and loyalties of the majority of the population. Indeed, if the state was unable to redeem the promise of material progress, it risked provoking opposition not merely from those who preached some brand of revolutionary socialism but from the traditional and/or religious right as well.

The wider political implications of the third world preoccupation with economic development were not immediately apparent. So long as the Soviet leadership showed little or no interest in decolonisation, it was the western, primarily the American view that mattered. The American fear of economic nationalism was not confined to western Europe. Just as Wilsonian liberals had seen national self-determination as being constitutively linked to democracy, so after 1945, their successors saw independence as a pre-requisite of

117

economic liberalism. They believed that independence was not merely good in and of itself, but that by dissolving the ties of empire, new states would be able to benefit from the gains from trade in a genuinely open market. Although it was their determination to combat the concept of trade preferences (particularly the British imperial system which was by far the most extensive) that led them to negotiate the GATT, it was their deep aversion to political interference in the market (for developmental or any other reasons) that led them to withdraw their support from the more wide-ranging International Trade Organisation (ITO). And it was primarily third world countries that had sought to accompany the proposals for trade liberalisation within the ITO with other measures, such as commodity price support schemes, specifically designed to advance their interests. The Americans believed that the exceptions to the GATT, particularly the infant industry exception (Article XVIII) provided sufficient safeguards to the legitimate development policies of the Asian, African and Latin American countries.

It was not merely western myopia and arrogance that accounted for the international neglect of development. No doubt there was no shortage of these unattractive qualities; but they were not confined to the west. Independence created a psychology of optimism as well as of hope. Non-alignment was the political expression, the five-year development plan, the economic expression of this mood. Development plans were not drawn up initially on the assumption of international financial assistance. Plan targets were set ambitiously high, on the mistaken assumption that new projects would be financed out of current earnings and reserves. The 'resource gap' – the idea of a calculable shortfall between a state's earning capacity and its 'legitimate' import requirements – was a later refinement of the development debate in the 1960s. India, whose experience in this regard was crucial, embarked on independence with ample reserves, the sterling balances accumulated as a result of the country's contribution to Britain's war effort. In the early 1950s, the Korean war led to a commodity price boom, which inflated the resources – and further fed the optimism – of many third world raw material producers.

The economics of non-alignment

The spectacular success of the Marshall Plan might have been expected to produce a rash of demands for similar financial assistance to Asia and Africa. It did not. Admittedly in later years liberals frequently invoked the precedent of Marshall Aid in debating the appropriate international response to intractable world problems; but those who argued that the right approach to the Arab–Israeli conflict, authoritarian rule in Latin America or famine in Africa, was to throw money at them, ignored both the nature of European economies and the essential political context of the original scheme. Not only was the Marshall Plan addressed to the problems of reconstruction rather than development, more importantly it was also conceived in the context of the cold war. A few third world countries (with particular fears or ambitions) were persuaded to align themselves with the west; but for the majority, national independence was interpreted as requiring a policy of non-alignment.[10]

So long as third world resources were buoyant, non-alignment seemed to have few economic implications, beyond a willingness to trade with any country regardless of ideological considerations, where this would advance the interests of the state concerned. It was just as well: while the Soviet leadership took little interest in the fate of the non-communist third world, there was no significant pressure on the United States' government to relax its doctrinal objections to direct public involvement in the economy, whether at home or abroad. Indeed, while the Soviet government appeared largely indifferent to post-colonial states, the United States was initially hostile to non-alignment, which it interpreted as a form of anti-western nationalism.[11]

The political landscape changed dramatically in 1955. Midway through its second five-year plan the Indian government had virtually exhausted its sterling balances. Consequently, it was faced with the alternatives of either abandoning its development strategy (or at least drastically scaling it down) or approaching the major powers for financial assistance. Simultaneously, the new Soviet leaders, Khrushchev and Bulganin, set out on a tour of Asia during which they announced that the Soviet Union was now prepared to assist the development of anti-imperialist but non-communist third world countries. In justification of the new policy, Soviet experts claimed to have identified a category of national democracies which had opted for a non-capitalist path to development.[12]

The conjunction of these two events finally put development on the international agenda. It also revealed the latent economic potential of a non-aligned foreign policy. The argument was as simple as it was seductive: if aid could be secured from both east and west, independence need not be compromised. Moreover, since the Soviet Union was only prepared to provide assistance for public sector projects, while the United States could be persuaded to assist private industry (as a means of combating the collectivisation of third world econo-mies), a degree of complementarity flowed from pursuing a non-aligned development strategy.

From the point of view of the recipients the major problems were practical rather than ideological. In the Indian case, which set the pattern, the Soviet commitment to the heavy industrial sector (where all new projects were reserved to the government) was soon matched by a coordinated programme of project and balance of payments support, organised by the Aid Indian Consortium under the auspices of the IMF.[13] But in India, as elsewhere, the demand for financial assistance from both east and west consistently outstripped supply.

The initial assumption on which western aid policies was based – that an injection of capital at strategic points in the economy would lead rapidly to the point of 'take off' and self-sustaining economic growth – proved to be false. Growth did occur, despite some notorious failures in 'aid-related' prestige projects.[14] But it led to an expansion rather than a contraction of import demand and so aggravated rather than eased the payment crises which foreign aid was meant to offset. The reason was that the local economy was seldom in a position to service new projects, so that a new demand was created for a steady flow of imported spare parts. Similarly, where a new industry was successfully established, secondary and tertiary industries grew up around it and these further added to the demand for imports. By the early 1960s it was already evident that the paradoxical consequence of treating economic development as a central political imperative in third world states, was to have engendered an increased economic dependence on the outside world. While this reinforced the pressures on governments to opt for national rather than liberal economic policies (and often led to outbursts of nationalistic frustration, par-ticularly against western multi-national corporations), the attachment of third world populations to their own governments was not notably increased.

Nation-building

With hindsight it seems obvious that, as a solution to the crisis of legitimacy in many post-colonial societies, the pursuit of economic development was seriously flawed. This was not merely because it suffered from the fallacies of economism, over-optimism about the potentialities of abstract economic planning, and the mistaken belief that peoples' fundamental loyalties are for sale. It was also because introspection should have led to greater caution. It is one thing to argue that in advanced industrial democracies political stability depends on affluence, that the realisable prospect of an improving material standard of living constitutes 'the Danegeld' by which the mass of the people are persuaded to endorse the social and political institutions of democracy and the market.[15] This belief is at least plausible and it may even be true. But why should one expect political stability – or respect for individual human rights – to be the outcome of a period of rapid economic development?

A people's loyalties may be purchased over the long, inter-generational, haul. Thus, the economic approach to 'nation-building' was flawed, but it was not wholly without foundation. Legitimate authority is not part of the natural order. In time people forget the past wrongs on which a particular political dispensation is established, just as they come to accept the national boundaries which emerged from ancient victories and defeats as being 'natural'. Indeed, how else could one account for the emergence of national consciousness in the centralised states of Europe, or anywhere else? But it is implausible to expect that a new social and economic order, which necessarily involves social dislocation and upheaval, can be achieved rapidly and painlessly. It is also probably implausible to believe that it can be achieved without a fairly high degree of coercion of a kind to which liberal theory is fundamentally opposed.[16]

However, from the point of view of third world governments it is not so obvious that their preoccupation with development was misconceived. Many leaders, like their western liberal supporters, may have entertained unrealistic hopes about what could be achieved. But except in those relatively few countries whose independent existence was under direct military threat, it is difficult to see what other justifications of rule they could have offered.

The struggle to preserve independence, as well as to rise in the international hierarchy, has always involved economic as well as military competition.[17] But, at all times, it has been the great powers, those which came out on top in the competition, that have set the standards by which success and failure is measured, and legitimacy extended or withheld from the relatively less successful. In the nineteenth century, not only were there still many countries whose rulers held their positions by prescriptive right, but in those where constitutional checks had been imposed on the government, such as Britain (still the major world power), the prevailing liberal ideology ruled out the idea of economic management. By 1945 this mixed regime had disintegrated; two superpowers competed for the attention of the third world. Moreover, each had a different vision of how to secure the peoples' sovereignty and its rightful patrimony. Both models – liberal pluralism and Marxism–Leninism – were built on the assumption that industrial society constituted the normal condition of modernity.[18] The pursuit of this condition was rarely perceived as an option, one possible policy amongst many: it was perceived as an imperative, a prerequisite for modern statehood, whose absence was both a challenge and a shame.

Industrialisation has become so firmly entrenched as the essential goal of modern states that the failure to make the transition from traditional to modern society (and by implication to create a national consciousness) can also be represented as a denial of a right. This claim is not as exaggerated as it may seem. In 1972 a second United Nations Convention on Human Rights extended the vocabulary of human rights from the civil and political rights of the liberal tradition to cover a much more extensive, if also much vaguer, list of social and economic rights. It was agreed, despite western opposition, to accommodate the interests and aspirations of both the eastern bloc and the third world.

JURIDICAL STATES AND 'FICTITIOUS' NATIONS

More generally, since 1945, the aspirations of third world nationalists have been endorsed, even underwritten, to an unprecedented degree. As Robert Jackson has pointed out, the contemporary international order is peculiarly tolerant of countries which are juridically sovereign (in the sense that they are recognised by other states and regularly occupy their seat at the United Nations) but which fail to meet the most fundamental empirical criteria of statehood as traditionally conceived.[19] More specifically, the existence of many such states does not signify the presence of a single civil society, and very often their governments fail either to guarantee the fundamental rights of the citizens or even to provide them with physical protection.

It is difficult to believe in Chad or Lebanon as even putative national states. At any other period in history they would have long since fallen prey to the ambitions of imperialist neighbours. Alternatively they would have disintegrated into smaller units more representative of the rival factions that in fact compete for power within the frontiers drawn by the colonial powers. However, territorial revision is currently regarded as anachronistic. As a result, states which are manifestly not viable in a political or economic sense, are nonetheless guaranteed in their juridical sovereignty by the international community. Since their rulers are unable to perform the most rudimentary tasks of civil government (such as disarming the population or raising sufficient

122

revenue from taxation to meet the running costs of the administration), it follows that these tasks must be undertaken by outside
powers, either collectively as a result of international agreement, or in
competition with one another in their effort to establish rival spheres
of interest.

Contemporary Afghanistan provides a vivid illustration of this
thesis. Afghanistan is an ancient country but with a deeply divided
political and social culture. The Soviet Union, which invaded the
country in 1979 (and installed a government of its own choice) has
been scarcely more successful than the British in the nineteenth
century in pacifying the countryside or disarming the tribesmen. Yet
the heroic resistance of the mujahideen has not succeeded in forging a
coherent national movement. Nor, any more than in Chad, has there
ever been a single Afghan civil society. It is the country's geo-political
existence rather than its political development that distinguishes it
from Chad. The Soviet Union has agreed to withdraw its forces, not
because they have been defeated by a determined and well-organised
national resistance but because they are tired of a situation which they
cannot control and which unnecessarily complicates relations between
Moscow and Washington.

The problem with such states for the rest of the world is that they
expose in an uncomfortably public and dramatic form the fiction that
the contemporary world order is built on nationality. It is not. It is built
on the separate territorial state, which may or may not preside over a
society in which national sentiment is strongly felt. Yet the current
political justification of the state requires that nations either exist or be
created. The point is not that nation-building must necessarily fail.
The third world contains a wide spectrum of states, some of which are
socially and politically stable. Some are also relatively successful
economically. The point is that once a state has been accepted
internationally, it has to be upheld, regardless of its government's
political and economic performance.

On the question of territorial revision modern international society
is more deeply conservative than it was before 1914: if Chad was
allowed to disappear because it failed to meet the empirical criteria for
state-hood, many other states, whose politics are dominated by
inter-ethnic or sub-national rivalries, would be at risk. There is a
virtually universal consensus that this must not be allowed to happen,
hence as we saw in chapter 4, the evolution of a conventional
interpretation of national self-determination. This interpretation con-
firms the national principle as the standard of legitimation in international society, but also confines the legitimate exercise of the

123

self-determination principle to the withdrawal of European imperial power. Once juridical sovereignty had been buttressed in this way, it was impossible to discriminate between 'real' and fictitious national states. All had to be supported.

A new political map was created by decolonisation, and subsequently guaranteed by the international community. The consequences were highly paradoxical. 'Nation-building' may not have failed in all cases, but economism as an approach to 'nation-building' has failed in most countries where it has been seriously attempted. In many, perhaps even the majority, politics are dominated not by nationalism but by ethnic or regional pressures for greater autonomy. Ethnic and religious divisions are exploited by local politicians, sometimes separately, and sometimes in combination, to force concessions from central governments. In such cases the pursuit of economic development exacerbates rather than weakens the centrifugal tendencies within society: the ultimate weapon of sub-national political movements is to threaten separatist agitation; the price that they demand for coming to terms with the centre is a greater share in the spoils.

In Africa the pattern emerged very soon after independence, producing what Ali Mazrui once called the re-tribalisation of African politics.[20] But it was equally prevalent in Asia and the Pacific.[21] The Indian state has been held together by a series of concessions to regional sentiment. In 1971, Pakistan was finally severed when a short-lived return to democracy threatened the permanent political and economic supremacy of West Pakistan over East Bengal. The conflicts in Sri Lanka between Tamils and Sinhalese, and in Fiji between the indigenous population and those of Indian descent, are similarly combusted of a mixture of ethnic rivalry and mutual suspicion. Fears about the demographic trends in each group, and their access to economic and other resources, in turn feed their antagonisms and undermine attempts to construct any overarching loyalty to the nation-state. There is nothing new in this process, except insofar as the governments of most third world countries seem even more intransigently opposed to solving the problem by federation or partition, than were, for example, Canada with respect to Quebec or Britain in relation to Ireland before 1921.

At the international level the pattern changes. The view of nationalism from New York, Geneva, Addis Ababa or wherever else governments conduct multilateral diplomacy, contrasts strikingly with the view from Delhi, Khartoum, Colombo or wherever the unity of the state and the authority of its government are at issue. One consequence of the domination of state politics by ethnic rivalries is that it allows the central government to monopolise the political vocabulary of nationalism and to manipulate its symbols on the international stage. By the end of the 1950s 'nation-building' had ceased to be merely a domestic concern of post-colonial governments. At the United Nations an anti-colonial alliance was forged, so that the political and economic aspirations of third world governments could be presented in terms of a series of claims on the international community. And, as a result of the cold war, the question of economic development became deeply embroiled in the rivalry and machi-nations of the great powers. The Non-Aligned Movement (NAM) maintained the political identity of third world states, independently of the cold war, but depended on it nonetheless to internationalise the question of development.

This combination had predictable results. On the one hand, organised ethnic or regional groups who were excluded from power, like the Tamils of Sri Lanka or the southern Sudanese, attempted to gain international support by exploiting great power rivalries and mobilising western liberal opinion through human rights and other pressure groups. On the other hand, governments attempted to deny them this access, while frequently arguing that political instability was a result of the marginalisation of the third world within the western dominated international economy. It followed, on this view, that the way to resolve problems of third world instability – and by implication to reduce the destructive potential of communal and sub-national passions – was to restructure the world economy so that third world participation would contribute positively to economic development. The identity of nationalism with anti-colonialism was preserved; or rather a way was found to continue the anti-colonial struggle by other means. It is to this attempt to buttress the official nationalism of third world governments by a campaign for international economic reform, that we now turn.

8 THE THIRD WORLD AND INTERNATIONAL SOCIETY

The idea of the third world has always been a chimera. The term was originally coined by western journalists and academic writers who needed a graphic image to reintroduce a degree of order into the post-imperial world.[1] They also sought to encapsulate an essential problem of post-colonial territories in relation to the western and communist powers. This problem was their subordination within an international hierarchy increasingly measured in terms of wealth as well as of military power. The term never lacked detractors, but it was nonetheless generally accepted by Asian, African, Caribbean and later Latin American leaders. Shiva Naipaul unwittingly revealed why.

> It is a flabby western concept lacking the flesh and blood of the actual ... a third world does not exist as such ... it has no collective and consistent identity except in the newspapers and amid the pomp and splendour of international conferences.[2]

Precisely so! Its utility in the political vocabulary of anti-colonial nationalism is largely explained by the access to the western media which membership of the third world gives, and the revisionist alliance which it conjures up for purposes of multilateral diplomacy.

A REVISIONIST ALLIANCE

The loose grouping of mostly new, Afro-Asian states origi-nated with the summit held in Bandung in 1955. Although many differ-ent interests and objectives were involved, its underlying collective purpose was to restructure international society. Independence was the essence of the nationalist position, so not surprisingly there was no talk at Bandung of either integration or supranational authority.

Afro-Asian objectives

Afro-Asian revisionism was based on three objectives which most third world leaders shared. These were non-alignment in the cold war, the elimination of all forms of colonialism and racism, and modernisation and economic development. The campaign to achieve these somewhat grandiose goals resulted in a process of rapid intellectual dispersal. Research institutes were established and university departments expanded to deal with the problems of post-colonial societies. Specialist national and international bureaucracies developed along separate lines in both the north and south. Those with expertise on political cooperation amongst the non-aligned, or who were active in the anti-apartheid movement, might know little or nothing about development economics. But the political class in most Asian and African countries nonetheless viewed the objectives as being inextricably linked. Non-alignment was necessary to avoid substituting one form of subordination for another; the abolition of colonialism and racism to insure against the possibility that the major powers might try to put the clock back in order to gain advantage in their own power-political struggles; and modernisation and development was necessary to give reality to their political independence and to enable the new states to maintain themselves in a self-help system.

Psychologically, the three objectives formed a coherent whole, although none of them, particularly the last, could be achieved by self-help alone. What gave the campaign its coherence, at least immediately following the transfer of power, was that most third world intellectuals and politicians saw these objectives as flowing from a broadly socialist, and therefore, 'progressive' analysis of the international situation. Non-alignment was originally as much a geo-political and strategic concept as a political one, but it recommended itself to many anti-colonial governments because they interpreted the western alliance as the military infrastructure of the world capitalist system.[3] This system they believed had been built by the exploitation of the third world and continued to prevent its development.

A similar analysis supported the other objectives. Despite the narrowly political nature of the anti-colonial struggle, the reality of continued economic domination and frustration was explained in terms of the continuing threat of neo-colonialism. By 1979, with the independence of Zimbabwe, Nkrumah's 'political kingdom' was firmly in the hands of Asian and African nationalists, leaving only the overthrow of the South African system of apartheid as a political target on which third world solidarity could be guaranteed. As more and more colonies became independent, their continued economic weaknesses exposed the flaw in his proposition.

Even with regard to South Africa the political and economic objectives were increasingly fused. The African National Congress (ANC), the major organised opposition to the South African government, shared most of the assumptions of the revisionist alliance about the economic basis of capitalist imperialism. Its Freedom Charter (1956) had included a provision for the state to take over the commanding heights of the economy as a necessary prerequisite to the dismantling of apartheid.[4] Indeed, in most economic theories of imperialism liberation was viewed as a prerequisite of development. Much of the literature on South Africa reflects this analysis: apartheid is represented as a form of internal colonialism.[5]

After a period of relative neglect the NAM was revived in the 1970s. However, the relative *détente* between the superpowers reduced the political salience of the cold war for the third world. Within the NAM the focus of attention increasingly shifted to the economic plight of the developing countries. From whatever angle the problem of third world participation in international society was approached, it seemed that the central issue arose out of its continued domination by western capitalism. Conflicting economic interests and philosophies (including the presence at most third world gatherings of some quite successful capitalist countries) were swept aside in an attempt to restructure the liberal world economy through collective pressure on the major powers.

Populists, radicals and reformers

Three strands of nationalist thought can be identified in many third world countries. First there is a populist nationalism which mostly manifests itself in ethnic agitation against the authority of the central state. It is populist in that it seeks to mobilise a community which is perceived to be hard done by in the existing political and economic dispensation (either because of relative deprivation or lack of proper reward). Populists exploit the political potential inherent in a shared folk culture, religion or ethnic identity and use whatever arguments are ready to hand without resort to any more general intellectual defence. South Asia abounds with examples of this kind of ethnic nationalism,[6] although in different versions it is to be found throughout the third world.

Populist agitation against the state finds virtually no place in the collective movements of the third world, although there are periodically reports of links between individual dissident movements. On the other hand, the second strand of third world nationalism has had a formative, if indirect, impact on the campaign for international

128

economic reform. It was developed by radical political economists whose target was the world capitalist system. Radical intellectuals were prominent in many anti-colonial movements but for the most part their economic understanding was primitive. Indeed, it was the failure of the early post-colonial governments to deliver what they promised that led to a more sustained radical critique of the inter- national system. Gradually, younger radicals in Asia and Africa joined forces with Latin American dependency theorists to explain the continuation of underdevelopment, and in many areas the absolute decline in living standards after independence.[7]

Radical intellectuals are frequently anti-goverment, but they have nonetheless been able to influence the official nationalism of third world countries for two reasons. First, the United Nations system provided many of them with employment and a suitably cosmopolitan and sympathetic base from which to develop a systemic critique of the world order. Secondly, although the critique itself does not employ cultural or linguistic categories, it rests implicitly on the assumption that third world countries are all structurally marginalised within the world capitalist system. Those who view the third world in this light generally ground their analysis in historical materialism, even though they break with orthodox Marxism at specific points. This common intellectual base line, in turn, allows them to take part in a discourse which is carried on in universities and research institutions across the world. Not only is the network of contacts thus established largely self-sustaining, but in the nature of the case, the political and pro- fessional classes of third world countries are likely to be recruited from amongst those who have been exposed at university to the radical critique, and its characteristic style of argument.

Are writers of this kind properly regarded as nationalists? It is difficult to answer this question because those who analyse the international system from a radical perspective do not adhere to a single doctrine or necessarily share the same presuppositions. Moreover, they seldom if ever present themselves as nationalists.

One group which deals with internal colonialism and the persist- ence of ethnic and national conflict explains these phenomena as resulting 'from a "cultural division of labour", in which members of an ethnic group are systematically assigned to a subordinate position within a given state or in the global context'.[8] They may sympathise with those brought up in nationalist politics, since they are the victims of vested interests and economic exploitation, but they clearly do not endorse the sentiments of the nationalists in their own terms. Indeed, they echo Marx in viewing nationalism as an ideological epiphenomenon which requires explanation and elucidation in terms of underlying economic realities. Similarly, those whose primary concern is with the causes of underdevelopment generally focus their analysis on the structure and working of capitalist imperialism, employing either some version of general systems theory or more often of dependency theory. In neither case is it clear that nationalist assumptions underpin their thought.

If radical intellectuals are nonetheless to be viewed as contributing to the collective nationalism of the third world, it is because of the logic of the positions they adopt rather than what they say about the subject themselves. Perhaps the most important point on which dependency theorists broke with orthodox Marxism was over the status of the periphery. Both Marxism and liberalism were implicitly, if not explicitly, Eurocentric. Liberals believed that only if the major capitalist countries maintained high rates of economic growth, could the more backward parts of the world be drawn into the expanding world market and so share in the general prosperity. Marxists originally held that revolution in the periphery could not precede revolution at the centre.[9]

Dependency theorists rejected these priorities and insisted that the impact of capitalist exploitation differed according to specific historic conditions in each part of the periphery. The idea of an international proletariat, sharing an historical consciousness and capable of being mobilised against the false consciousness of the nation, is thus demolished. Presumably the class of peasants and workers which is represented as the victim of oppression and exploitation is a 'national' or at least a territorial class, although they seldom employ the category of nation-state in their analysis.

Two further pieces of internal evidence support this conclusion. First, the capitalist class in peripheral countries is often portrayed as fulfilling a *comprador* or middle-man position for international capital. In other words, it is viewed as a kind of fifth column whose interests are identified with the industrial west against the 'real' interests of their own people. But if there is a people, which can be betrayed in this way, it must have an identity: the strong presumption is that the country belongs to the mass of the population which has been historically contained within the state's frontiers and which therefore forms a legitimate but oppressed historical community. If this is not a national community what is it? Secondly, dependency theorists who extend their analysis to prescribe ways out of the trap of underdevelopment have often argued in favour of delinking peripheral countries from the world capitalist economy. Very few third world

130

governments have been inclined to follow this advice, but if they were to do so, it would clearly require the adoption of a rigorous autarkic policy of the kind discussed in chapter 5.

The official class in most third world countries is unlikely to be sympathetic to those parts of the radical critique in which the government and its administration are represented as part of the machinery of capitalist oppression. Nor are they likely to favour development strategies which seek to sever their links with either the major powers or international organisations and development agencies. Since they see themselves as the true representatives of the nation-in-the-making, and spend their professional lives within a world which is shaped by international debate and negotiation, not surprisingly they have adopted a utilitarian approach to radical arguments. They have adopted those parts of the analysis which point to the structural handicaps under which third world countries operate within the international division of labour, while themselves seeking, by negotiation, to reform the liberal order in ways which will accommodate the interests and aspirations of third world governments.

If the central objective of populists is to reassert cultural authenticity against the centralising tendencies of the westernised state, and that of radicals to break with the world capitalist order, the reformers have attempted to make empirical reality conform more closely with the juridical equality of states. Reformers habitually argue by domestic analogy. They seek to treat international society as if it were an enlarged version of a social democratic welfare state. In the latter case income is redistributed through progressive taxation and citizens have positive entitlements to welfare; in the latter, reformers argue for resource transfers, preferential trade and pricing arrangements and the transfer of technology 'as of right', rather than at the political discretion of the major powers.[10]

The essence of any reform movement is that the process of argument and debate (and even on some issues confrontation with the defenders of the *status quo*) will not be carried to the point of an open challenge to the system as a whole. The most that reformers can do is to warn of the likely consequences if adjustments to the system are not made in time. They cannot actively seek to bring about these consequences, because they are as deeply opposed to them, on grounds of both interest and conviction, as those with whom they negotiate. It follows from the nature of their predicament that, if they are to succeed, reformers need to be acutely sensitive to changes in the environment in which they operate, and opportunities that such changes may offer. Those who enjoy a margin of wealth or power can

131

afford to be wasteful and inattentive; those who must rely on per-
suasion to achieve their ends must be watchful and husband their
resources.

For the most part, third world reformers have conducted their
campaign in accordance with these maxims. When they have deviated
from them, it has been because either their intellectual debt to the
radicals, or their own misreading of changes in the international
environment, have led them to adopt a more stridently nationalist and
confrontational posture than was consistent with diplomatic negotiation. Thus, for a short period after the quadrupling of the oil price by
OAPEC (and OPEC) in 1973–4, third world objectives were presented
as categorical demands for a radically restructured New International
Economic Order (NIEO). These demands met with a predictably
negative response from the western industrial countries whose
governments were expected to surrender their oligopolistic control
over the institutions of the world economy. Progress was only
resumed after the confrontational stance was abandoned, and third
world governments (and their western supporters) emphasised the
essentially reformist nature of the NIEO and its appeal to the long-run
self-interest of the industrial powers.

By virtue of their programme – to reform the liberal international
economy – third world negotiators borrowed eclectically from the
mercantalist, nationalist and liberal traditions of economic thought.
The objective of 'self-reliance' as a means of reducing dependence on
the industrial west, derives from mercantilist assumptions about the
nature and purposes of the state. The justification of industrial and
service protection for developmental purposes derives from the 'infant
industry' argument first developed by Hamilton and List. The attempt
to secure improved access to western markets by the removal of the
'escalating tariffs' imposed by western countries on third world exports
is fully consistent with neo-classical trade theory. The familiarity of
such arguments was an asset in negotiation: just as anti-colonial
nationalism orginally depended heavily on an alliance between the
nationalists in the colonies and their liberal and social democratic supporters in the metropolitan countries, so the third world reform movement depended on an alliance between those responsible for
development policies in third world governments and their supporters
in North America and western Europe.

Developments within the economics profession in the West
reinforced the domestic analogy on which the third world reform
programme was based: the growth of Keynesian welfare economics
after 1945 fed the parallel growth of development economics. Both

shared the same normative bias, namely, to put economic rationality to the service of economic reform and social justice. Depending on the time, the speaker and his audience, official north–south economic relations were variously described as a north–south conflict or a north–south dialogue; but however described, both the definition of the development problem and the strategies which were advanced to resolve it, were worked out jointly by a transnational 'community' of development experts.

The major achievement of the reform movement was the establishment of the United Nations Conference on Trade and Development (UNCTAD) in 1964. The UNCTAD is a multilateral organisation, allegedly designed to serve the international community as a whole, but from the start it has acted to advance the interests of the third world within the liberal international economy. Indeed, in some respects, the UNCTAD secretariat provides the kinds of services for the Group of 77 (research into common problems, data collection and the formulation of potential strategies for policy coordination) that the OECD provides for the industrial democracies.

THE LOGIC AND STRUCTURE OF THE REFORM PROGRAMME

The third world agenda for international economic reform has not changed much in thirty years, although different aspects of the programme have gained prominence at different times. The basic demands have been for an increased flow of concessional aid from north to south; improved (preferably free) access for third world exports into northern (primarily western) markets and special arrangements to stabilise (and arguably enhance) the prices of their commodity exports. The underlying rationale, which integrated these demands, was heavily influenced by the radical critique of world capitalism. Its most authoritative formulation was by Raul Prebisch, the Argentinian economist who served as the first Secretary-General to the UNCTAD.

Most radical political economists argue that the world economy is structured in such a way that not only do the gains from trade accrue disproportionately to the north, but that under modern capitalist conditions, it is not possible to reverse this trend. In his report to the first UNCTAD, *Towards a New Trade Policy for Development*,[11] Prebisch accepted the first of these propositions but not the second. In so doing he adopted the traditional stance of liberal nationalists, albeit adjusting a nineteenth-century argument to suit twentieth-century conditions. On this view, nationalism and liberalism are allies on the side of freedom, self-determination and rationality, against the powers of custom, determinism and unreason. The adjustment which is necessary to reassert the rationality of the nationalist case concerns the area in which free (or political) will is capable of influencing events. Since the reform movement's chances of success are critically dependent on the persuasive power of this new liberalism, it is worth exploring its intellectual background and logical structure in more detail.

The new liberalism

Classical liberalism is only minimally concerned with the conditions under which individual freedom is possible. Some attention is given to the fate of industrial latecomers who may need initial protection before they can compete on equal terms with established producers. In time, the list of public goods, which have to be financed out of public funds, was extended from defence to utilities (e.g. drainage and other public health facilities) which, since they could not easily be consumed in private, were inherently unlikely to be provided by the market. But, in general, liberals were concerned with the cognitive equality of human beings (each should count for one and no more than one) and with the creation of a legal and institutional order within which individual rights would be equally protected. They had no concept of subsistence rights and no coherent rebuttal to the objection that equality before the law or freedom of speech was of no use to the starving or the destitute.[12]

The GATT originally reflected this liberal background picture. All contracting parties, regardless of their stage of development, were assumed to be capable of negotiating as sovereign states on the basis of the MFN principle. However, once development was accepted as an international political question, and not merely a fortuitous outcome of market forces, the conditions of liberty were inevitably called into question. By the early 1960s the proposition that there could be no equality of treatment between unequals was widely accepted. In north–south relations it was successfully invoked by third world governments to obtain a revision of the GATT. A new chapter was added to the agreement devoted to the special problems of the developing countries.[13] Its central provision allows them to participate in tariff negotiations, and to benefit from all the concessions obtained under the MFN principle, without having to offer anything in return. Non-reciprocity was thus substituted for reciprocity as the cardinal principle of north–south economic relations.

134

Those who seek to negotiate on the basis of non-reciprocity face a major practical obstacle. They are entirely dependent on the force of public opinion and the goodwill of their opponents, who are called upon to make the concessions. The experience of the developing countries in the Kennedy Round of GATT negotiations demonstrated that, even when good will is present, the outcome may do little to advance their interests. In this case, it was so difficult to secure agreement between the major economic powers, that the interests of the developing countries, which had nothing themselves to offer, were inevitably brushed aside.[14]

The terms of trade argument

For third world governments, the UNCTAD was valued because it established a permanent institution which could both publicise their development needs and mobilise international support for the reform programme. In this respect the Prebisch Report played a crucial role. Its central argument was simple. Prebisch maintained that there had been a long-term secular decline in the terms of trade of the Group of 77 countries as a whole – that is in the price ratio of their raw material exports to their imports of manufactures and capital goods. Further, he maintained that for structural reasons (e.g. the strength of organised labour in the industrialised countries and its weakness in the third world) this trend was unlikely to be reversed by market forces. It followed that, if the third world was to recapture its rightful share of the gains from trade, and to remain committed to a relatively open liberal world economy, the natural bias of the market in favour of the strong would have to be corrected by deliberate international intervention.[15]

Power liberates: structure constrains. This was the hidden assumption, which was seldom commented upon but provided the link between the radical critique of the capitalist economy and the third world reform programme. In other words the argument assumed that while third world countries were caught in a poverty trap, which was not of their own making but from which there was no independent escape, the industrial countries were not similarly constrained. They were, therefore, in a position to introduce legal and market changes in the world's trading and monetary systems. What was required was an act of political will.

The validity of the argument need not detain us here. The governments of the industrial countries never accepted it and after 1974 it could only be salvaged by omitting oil from the list of products on which the original calculations had been based. The strength of the 'terms of trade' argument did not lie in the economic analysis on which it was based. It lay in the accuracy in which it reflected nationalist perceptions and experience throughout much of the third world. Economists who constructed time series stretching back into the colonial period, designed to show that there was no permanent, one way, movement in the relation of raw material to manufactured prices, missed the essential point. In the political lifetime of most third world leaders, particularly those of the poorest and most dependent countries, there had indeed been a decline. They were seldom interested in the good time that had allegedly existed before the nationalist period or in long-term projections. The immediate situation they faced was one in which they had to rely on a narrow range of traditional raw material exports, the demand for which was very often inelastic, and constantly rising demands for foreign exchange to cover essential imports.

The logic of the 'terms of trade' argument could be extended in two directions. The first led to demands for a set of reforms to the liberal economic order which would allow it to make a positive contribution to third world development. These demands required the industrial countries to extend the welfare principle of progressive income distribution to the international sphere; to live up to their liberal pretensions by dismantling restraints on trade which discriminated against third world exports; and to introduce a system of positive discrimination in their favour. Thus much effort was devoted to persuading the OECD countries to commit 1 per cent of their GNP to development assistance (later reduced to 0.7 per cent in an effort to operationalise the commitment and make it more effective) and to negotiating the General Specialised Preference Scheme (GSP).[16] The reintroduction of preferential trade was sold to doctrinaire liberals in the United States on the grounds that if all the industrial countries were to grant preferences toward developing countries, at least the spirit of non-discrimination – the bedrock of the liberal trade order – would be preserved.

The nationalist element in the third world reform movement can be seen clearly if its underlying rationale is compared to that of the Bretton Woods system and GATT. In order to restore the liberal international order after 1945 it had been necessary to make specific concessions to the principle of *national* welfare (and in particular to recognise the state's commitment to pursue full employment policies). The aim was to combine Keynesian economic policies at home with the international policies favoured by the classical economists. Third world reformers reversed the priorities, or rather urged the extension of the welfare principle and Keynesian economic management from the domestic to the international sphere so far as north–south relations were concerned. The new criticism of the liberal order, like the old, was based on the priority of national over international interests. In the industrial world the concern had been to prevent the new institutional system from frustrating government policies in support of full employment and welfare programmes – after 1945 these were increasingly accepted as defining the identity between the state and the national community. In the third world the object of the critique was to engage the international community in their national development plans. This could not happen without an act of political will.

Multilateralism was the device through which the third world countries collectively tried to bend the international community to their will. It was also the only form of diplomacy which had any hope of overcoming a major objection to the involvement of the major powers in third world development. If these powers had a responsibility to contribute to the development process, what was to distinguish their legitimate efforts to discharge this responsibility from intervention designed to further their own power political interests? The radical political economists claimed that, within the capitalist world order, no such distinction was possible. Indeed, they viewed most north–south diplomacy as a trick by which northern governments attempted to coopt third world elites.

The reformers, however, clung stubbornly to the domestic analogy on which they had pinned their hopes. In some industrial democracies left-wing and popular pressure had forced modifications in liberal doctrine to make room for positive rights alongside the traditional negative freedoms. Why should not 'progressive' international opinion, backed by the numerical supremacy of the third world states in international organisations, similarly force modifications in the established international order? In this case the changes would need to accommodate multilaterally agreed entitlements alongside non-interference in the domestic affairs of the states and non-discrimination in international trade, the two cardinal principles of liberal international thought. I shall return to this question in the final section of this chapter.

The second extension of the 'terms of trade' argument was directed to national rather than international policies. The argument could be used to support import substitution as the appropriate development strategy at the national level. Although internationally, the thrust of the third world campaign was to open up western markets to their exports and to raise their prices, both necessity and national aspiration worked in the opposite direction so far as western participation in third world markets was concerned. The attempt to accelerate planned development was almost invariably accompanied by balance of payments crises. In the short run, declining terms of trade meant that governments were constantly short of foreign exchange to cover essential imports. Necessity, therefore, forced them to impose strict import licensing regimes regardless of their ideological predispositions. In the GATT the infant industry exception to the MFN rule was seldom invoked, partly because it subjected the government to tiresome procedures of international surveillance, but largely because it was unnecessary. Most third world governments were forced to impose import restrictions in order to honour their outstanding debts.

Import substitution was also considered necessary for another reason. The 'terms of trade' argument was an attempt to explain the change in the structure of the global economy: during the 1950s manufactures had replaced raw materials as the dynamic sector of world trade. If third world countries were to reap the benefits of this shift it followed that national development would need to involve a process of industrial diversification.[17] Indeed, the ultimate justification of the international campaign for special preferences was to enable them to participate in manufacturing trade – from this point of view the GSP was a kind of generalised and internationalised extension of the infant industry argument. It made no sense, so ran the argument, for the western powers to provide financial assistance for third world industrialisation and then to block their entry into world markets.

Finally, the case for import substitution was strengthened by the argument that export industries require a strong domestic market from which to expand and on which they can fall back in hard times. Much has been made recently of the advantages of export-led growth over import-substitution. But leaving aside those countries whose internal market is so small that it cannot possibly support a domestically oriented industry, this argument overlooks the fact that the successful industrialising countries – Korea is the prime example – preceded their assault on world markets with a period in which the domestic market was both nurtured and heavily protected against foreign competition.

Beyond these technical considerations, the import substitution strategy corresponded to the political aspirations of most third world nationalists. Moreover, this correspondence could generally be observed in regimes which professed to be guided by a liberal pluralist ideology as well as those which had opted for socialism. In countries like Cuba, Vietnam or Algeria, the expropriation (or very strict control) of foreign private investments and the state control of trade was considered an essential prerequisite of post-colonial development. But even in capitalist, or proto-capitalist countries such as Kenya or Nigeria the governments were committed not merely to industrial diversification but also to indigenisation, sometimes by reserving certain sectors for development by nationals, or by demanding a substantial (often majority) share of the equity in joint ventures with foreign enterprises. India and a few other countries with large domestic markets adopted a mixed regime combining aspects of both these strategies.

The nationalist preference for import substitution was most clearly visible in the service sector. Unlike commodities, services have to be tailored to the particular needs of a community and provided directly at the point of consumption. Foreign ownership, therefore, drama-tises the absence of economic control and independence. In many cases more immediate pressures for indigenisation were probably decisive: sectors such as banking and insurance were already heavily dependent on local labour and know-how, so that there was little to be lost by taking them into public ownership. So long as they were not dependent on imported technology, the development of a parastatal service sector could also be used as an employment outlet for the rapidly expanding educated class, and as a reward system for loyalty to state and/or party. In this context political and commercial criteria for deciding the national interest would not necessarily be the same.

The third world assault on the conference system which tradi-tionally controlled world shipping had a different but parallel aim. A national shipping line, such as the Black Star Line which the Israelis helped Nkrumah set up in Ghana, was a dramatic symbol of a new state's independence and of its determination to take part in the world economy, on its own behalf rather than by permission of the leading maritime powers. At the same time countries that were habitually short of foreign exchange were understandably hostile to a system which exercised oligopolistic control over the world shipping market, and from which they were excluded.

- EVALUATION

So much for the structure and logic of the reformers' argu-ment. What of the outcome? No definitive answer to this question is possible. In the sense that both the north–south debate and multilateral diplomacy continue, the jury is still out. Nor is this the place to conduct an analysis of Asian, African, and Latin American development strategies. In terms of the impact of collective diplomacy on both the liberal world order and on third world nationalism, however, a tentative interim conclusion is possible. It is that as the major western powers reduced their commitment to multilateralism after 1979, there has been an enforced retreat from the reform programme and an apparent revival of economic liberalism not only in the industrial west but in many of the third world countries also. In many cases this revival is essentially a result of conditions imposed by the IMF in return for debt relief – in Africa virtually every government is engaged in some form of structural adjustment programme[18] – but it also reflects the widespread acknowledgement within the third world itself that many national development policies have been misconceived.

The conclusion is paradoxical because it was the attempt to reconstruct and reinforce the liberal economic order against the forces of economic nationalism that led to the establishment of international economic institutions as a framework for multilateral diplomacy. It is also paradoxical that in many developing countries the attempt to return certain sectors of the economy to the market has sharpened the internal debate about the appropriate policies for preserving (or constructing) a national identity and developing the national economy. Governments which could previously shelter behind the third world consensus on the need for world economic reform, are increasingly vulnerable to criticism and attack from ethnic and other separatist groups which in various ways find themselves bypassed in the process of modernisation.

The weakening of the revisionist alliance had both internal and external origins. An alliance which asserted the primacy of economic nationalism over the dominant liberal order was probably bound to founder eventually under the weight of its own inner contradictions. National interests conflict, almost by definition, and such conflicts will be intensified when countries produce essentially the same or similar commodities and compete for access to the same markets. The articulation of a common interest for the Group of 77 (which in fact includes about 120 countries) is a formidable task even in propitious circumstances. During a period of world-wide recession, when the temptation to break ranks increases, it is virtually impossible. In these circumstances, governments are likely to exploit any special economic, political or geographical advantage they may enjoy to maintain their share of world export markets, regardless of the impact on the reform programme as a whole.

140

Three factors helped to conceal this harsh reality in the twenty years following the Bandung Conference. The first, and most important, was the relative buoyancy of the world economy; it was during this period that the developing countries complained most loudly that the GATT and the Bretton Woods system were rich country clubs designed to preserve the *status quo*; but it was also a time when they were most successful in generating political interest in third world development amongst OECD governments. Rapid economic growth in the industrial economies enabled them to take a relatively longer term and optimistic view of global economic integration than in the decade following the energy crisis of the mid-1970s.

Secondly, because the reforms they demanded required action by the western powers only, solidarity was relatively cost-free to the Group of 77. There was some, largely rhetorical, acknowledgement of the importance of south–south cooperation, and the need to construct a system of collective self-reliance. But although some programmes were developed and there was a steady, if modest, growth of such trade the possibilities were limited and in most cases the practical constraints overwhelming.

The approach which was adopted within the Group of 77 involved putting together a package of demands according to the principle of the highest common denominator. In other words, there would be something in it to suit all interests and, therefore, no incentive for any country to defect. This is is the opposite technique to that which must be adopted by any group of countries which genuinely attempts to integrate its economic activities. The residual economic nationalism of the EEC countries notoriously forces them to operate under the principle of the lowest common denominator; integration proceeding accordingly at the pace of the slowest and most reluctant member.

Thirdly, despite the maximalist demands, progress did not have to be made on all fronts simultaneously. It is not unduly cynical to suggest that, for the narrowly political purpose of continuing the anti-colonial struggle into the post-colonial era, it was sufficient to demonstrate third world solidarity at regular intervals. The summit meetings of the NAM, the meetings of the UNCTAD and even the two-yearly Commonwealth summits, provided opportunities for this collective demonstration of nationalist aspirations.

Between these set piece meetings, at which there was frequently an appearance of confrontation rather than negotiation, detailed work was carried out by officials on whatever aspect of the programme could be translated from utopian rhetoric into practical proposals for change. Thus, for much of the 1960s, north–south negotiations were dominated by the GSP scheme. The Group of 77 was able to give the scheme its full support because it represented a potential gain for all countries even if only a few (i.e. those with a manufacturing sector) would be able to benefit from it in the foreseeable future. Similarly, the industrial countries were able to concede special trade preferences because the introduction of an element of positive discrimination into the liberal trade order was designed to preserve the principle of open market trading, not to replace it with a system of managed markets. The fact that the anticipated cost was small also meant that they did not have to worry greatly about pressure from domestic producers whose interests would be adversely affected. At the diplomatic level, the price was well worth paying as a hedge against any widespread third world defection to bilateralism, the expropriation of western assets and an increasingly hostile attitude to private foreign investment.

The climax of these third world efforts at international economic reform came with the sixth and seventh special sessions of the United Nations General Assembly in 1976/7. These meetings, which witnessed the launching of the campaign for the NIEO, also marked the point from which the third world's collective nationalism began to decline. The dramatic quadrupling of the oil price in 1973/4 was widely welcomed in the third world despite the fact that for the majority the immediate effect was to saddle them with a crippling debt.[19] The revolt of the oil producers was welcomed because for the first time a group of developing countries, acting together, had changed the balance of economic power in the world economy. There were also exaggerated hopes that their success would have a demonstration effect amongst the producers of other raw materials, and an even more exaggerated optimism about the strength of the Arab commitment to the rest of the third world. The optimists hoped that once the oil producing countries had captured a major share of world resources they would translate this into political leadership for the third world as a whole.

For a time it seemed as if these hopes and calculations were well founded. The governments of the industrial democracies were undoubtedly shaken. The Americans tried unsuccessfully to organise a consumers' cartel to fight off the challenge of third world producers. After the two United Nations special sessions had dramatised the depth of the north–south divide, the industrial countries attempted to defuse the conflict. The French first organised a dialogue on a selective basis. The hope was that by limiting the membership of the conference it would be possible to identify areas of fruitful negotiation to replace the rhetorical invective to which north–south relations were frequently reduced.[20] The Paris meeting may have contributed to mutual confidence, but it produced nothing concrete. The final set piece negotiation again took place under the auspices of UNCTAD and therefore between the Group of 77 as a whole and Group B – the negotiating committee of the western industrial countries.

The negotiations on UNCTAD's Integrated Programme on Commodities (IPC) provided a similar focus to the development debate in the late 1970s as had those on the GSP in the 1960s. Once again the Group of 77 gained strength by presenting an ostensibly common front. Whether this front could have been maintained for long is more questionable: had the Fund been agreed in the form originally envisaged some of the economically more advanced countries, which were themselves net importers of raw materials, stood to lose.

More seriously, from the standpoint of collective nationalism the IPC offered two hostages to fortune. The Group of 77 had originally envisaged a new institution with very substantial resources of its own, and the capacity to intervene in commodity markets and set up international commodity agreements (ICAs) on its own initiative. While the main purpose of the Fund was to create buffer stocks, a 'second window' was added in the form of financial aid into alternative uses, development research etc. This was necessary, under the highest common denominator formula, to satisfy those countries, mainly in Africa, whose principal export commodities did not lend themselves technically to buffer stock management.

Finally, the Fund was to be very largely under third world management and would therefore constitute a major break with other international economic institutions which remained under the control of the industrial states. Opinion within the western camp on the desirability of the Fund was mixed, and none of these proposals, particularly the last, was greeted with any intellectual enthusiasm. The Common Fund, in its emasculated form, was finally agreed in 1980 but proved to be stillborn.[21]

The second hostage to fortune followed from the first. Having committed themselves to negotiate on commodity pricing in the aftermath of the energy crisis, the western powers engaged in damage limitation. By the time it finally emerged, the Common Fund had been effectively emasculated, probably to the relief of some of the Group of 77 as well as the west. However, it was the world economic recession, at the beginning of the 1980s (and the return of a buyer's market for most raw materials) that sealed the fate of the third world reform movement.

The recession provided the international background for a retreat from Keynesian economics (and from Keynesian optimism about the managed economy) throughout the capitalist world. The United States, in particular, also sounded a retreat from multilateralism. This immediately undermined the basic assumption on which the third world reform movement was based, namely that numerical voting power could partially offset relative weakness in economic and military capabilities. For this to happen, western public opinion would first have to be mobilised and then persuaded of the justice of third world demands. Once western governments no longer provided an automatic and receptive audience for these demands, refused to contemplate global negotiations outside the GATT, and downgraded their commitment to development, both tasks were rendered virtually impossible. The framework of multilateral diplomacy was not abandoned, and in the context of the third world debt crisis there has even been some modest revival of interest in it by the United States. But the momentum has been lost, and it is difficult to foresee under what circumstances it may be revived.

If the attempted reconciliation between welfare nationalism and the liberal economic order has proved unstable, as was suggested in chapter 6, no wonder that the third world attempt to extend the welfare concept to the international community has collapsed altogether. Despite the complex interdependencies (and dependencies) of an increasingly integrated world market, a system of nation-states (and would-be nation-states) remains a stubbornly self-help system. In such a system certain 'rules of the game' (i.e. the observable but implicit rules of calculation and prudence) may emerge. No doubt they will also change from time to time in response to economic, military and technological developments. But the liberal attempt to construct an international society, in which the diplomacy of pressure and force will be progressively replaced by a rule-based diplomacy insulated from mercantilist and nationalist rivalries, seems doomed to fail.

144

CONCLUSION

The two central claims of this book can be briefly stated. First, the primacy of the national idea amongst contemporary political principles has modified the traditional conception of an international society but has not replaced it. Second, there is no immediate prospect of transcending the national idea, either as the principle of legitimisation or as the basis of political organisation for the modern state. Hence, for the time being, international society cannot develop in ways which are inconsistent with the continued existence of separate national states. Islands of supra-national authority may arise here and there, but the principle of popular sovereignty will not easily translate into supra-nationalism in general.

To summarise the argument which supports these claims let us return to the three questions that were raised in the Introduction. What is meant by international society? On what normative principles is the idea of international society based? How has nationalist doctrine, and more broadly the national idea, influenced its evolution? I shall consider each briefly in turn.

The original conception of international society has survived into the modern world with its basic structure intact. It is a conception of a society of states which recognise each other's sovereignty, engage in regular diplomatic relations with one another and uphold international law. The theoretical alternatives to this scheme have not materialised. These are some form of world empire or dominion, or the evolution of political arrangements designed with reference to a community of mankind, rather than separate national communities. The separate state has shown an equally stubborn resistance to withering away, as Marx and his immediate followers hoped it would, as it has to retreating to the parsimonious but universal Republican form favoured by Kantian liberals.

International cooperation is always and everywhere dependent on the prior recognition of the sovereignty principle. When modern states collectively endorse a solidarist ideology – as the new African states did with Pan-Africanism in the 1960s – they define it in a way which reasserts the primacy of the state in the event of a conflict between the national interest and any wider obligation. And when the government of a single state elects to ignore the conventions of international society and to base its foreign policy on a unilateral interpretation of either a common ideology or its own rights, it finds it correspondingly difficult to solicit international support. This is the fundamental explanation of Libya's diplomatic isolation within the Arab world and Africa, as it is of post-revolutionary Iran's in international society as a whole. It is also the reason why irridentist states find it difficult to attract allies.

It may reasonably be objected that the sovereignty principle provides weak states with scant protection against the predatory interventions of the powerful. Both the United States and the Soviet Union have not hesitated to equate their own interests with some universal imperative – the defence of the 'free world' in the one case, of the socialist commonwealth in the other – when it suited them to do so. Nor have lesser states been much more scrupulous in the exercise of self-restraint when they have found themselves involved in international disputes.

This is a forceful objection, but from the standpoint of international society, it needs to be placed in context. In the original conception, the balance of power was generally acknowledged to be one of the institutions of international society. Indeed, in the view of many realists it was the primary institution which provided the minimum of order on which the whole edifice rested. Admittedly, one result of the attempt – enshrined in the United Nations Charter – to confine the legitimate use of force to self-defence, has been to remove war from its place as an institution of international society. Instead it is regarded as the primary evidence of its breakdown. Nonetheless, this is an area in which state practice sadly lags behind the development of international law. Although great as well as small powers must these days resort to moral justification for the use of force, there is little doubt that they still consider themselves as enjoying special rights to match their ultimate responsibility for world order.

If the waging of war is one aspect of the idea of international society which has been modified in the twentieth century, the arrangements for the conduct of peaceful relations amongst states is another. The original conception envisaged a society of sovereigns who held certain principles and practices in common. They saw no need for an institutional infrastructure in the modern sense. Indeed, both their interpretation of sovereignty to include the right to wage war as an act

146

of policy, and the two economic strategies open to them – mercantilism and classical liberalism – precluded such an infrastructure. By contrast, twentieth-century experience of war and peace not only brought about modifications in the traditional idea of international society but ensured that an attempt would be made to operationalise the idea by giving it a permanent institutional form.

The attempt to create a new multilateral system of collective security, although unsuccessful, nonetheless expanded the conception of international society to include multilateralism in general. The United Nations Organization, and its affiliates, continued the process of institutionalisation begun under the League: since 1945, very few issues in international relations, particularly in the economic and social fields, have escaped multilateral debate and negotiation. To the idea of an international society of states has been added the notion of an international agenda, a set of problems which it is their collective duty to keep under review, and eventually to resolve.

So much for the idea of international society. What of the principles on which it is based and which are embedded within it? Those on which the original conception was based have already been alluded to since they are all derivations of the sovereignty principle. A society of sovereigns came into being when they acknowledged each other's political supremacy, including the right to determine the beliefs of their respective subjects. This right has been formally abandoned in the light of one of the major modifications to the idea of international society. I shall return shortly to this modification – the entrenchment of human rights on the international agenda. Here the point is that *cuius regio eius religio*, the original principle, bears a strong family resemblance to its contemporary successor, the principle of non-interference in the domestic affairs of other states.

Two other principles underpin contemporary international society, as they did the original conception. The first is the principle of consent as the basis of international law. This body of law has expanded continuously to keep pace with the enormously increased volume and scope of international interactions, but the sovereignty principle continues to set limits to the legal sanctions that can be imposed to uphold it. International law thus continues to depend on the binding status which governments accord to treaties, on the fear of reciprocal reprisals, and on self-policing.

The second principle which has survived the modification of international society is diplomatic immunity. Modern diplomats are in many respects indistinguishable from other servants of the state. Their day to day work is increasingly concerned with the administration of complex economic or military programmes and the resolution of conflicts of interest through negotiation. But, when they serve abroad, their privileges and immunities still derive from their symbolic not their functional role, i.e. from the fact that they are the representatives of a sovereign state. In practice more attention is no doubt paid to the plenipotentiaries of the United States, the Soviet Union or China than to those of Mexico, Bulgaria or Thailand. But, in a formal sense, in any capital of the world, they are all the representatives of sovereign powers in a society of equals.

The modifications and additions to the original conception of international society stem from the acceptance of new principles. These are all derived, in the first instance, from liberal theory. Since the idea of international society is not exclusively the preserve of liberals, it is important to emphasise that the derivation is *intellectual* not practical or political. The claim is that certain Enlightenment principles have become so firmly embedded in modern consciousness that, as Ortega Y Gasset argued, they established the language of political argument – and its idiom – even for those who might wish to repudiate them. Not all allegedly liberal principles have achieved this bipartisan, a-political, international status. The attempt to transform international society by means of multilateral diplomacy, into a kind of surrogate welfare state, has conspicuously failed.

The liberal principles which have been universally endorsed, at least at the international level, are all concerned with the idea of human rights. From the egalitarian conception of a humanity, commonly endowed with natural rights to life, liberty and the pursuit of happiness, derives the necessity, only grudgingly and partially admitted by states, that individual human beings are the ultimate source of political authority, and that, therefore, their rights must be publicly acknowledged within international society. It is still a society of states but the states now belong to the people. Governments which torture some of the people for their political or religious beliefs, or blatantly exploit them for the narrow advantage of an unrepresentative political clique, must be accountable for their actions. However far short of this ideal state practice falls, it is the logic behind the United Nations human rights regime. It is also a logic that no one is prepared to deny. The crucial document is appropriately entitled *The Universal Declaration of Human Rights*.

Two other principles, also derived from the same Enlightenment seed-bed, have been grafted onto the idea of international society. These are the restriction on the legitimate use of force, and the duty of states to recognise the social, economic and cultural rights of their people, in addition to the original list of civil and political rights. Arguably neither is as firmly enthroned in the contemporary conception of international society as the other principles we have discussed. The attempt to constrain governments in their use of force continues to fall foul, as we have seen, of the appeal of the balance of power as an enabling concept in the foreign policies of the strongest states. More generally, it has been repeatedly undermined by the impossibility of reaching an uncontested definition of the concept of aggression. The idea of social and economic rights is seriously weakened by the impossibility of specifying how these rights are to be delivered, and by whom, in circumstances which often lie beyond the control of governments or even of international society as a whole. Nonetheless the fact that no government will admit that its foreign policy is aimed at military aggrandisement and that they all acknowledge the need for economic cooperation strongly supports the inclusion of these principles in our account of the modified idea of an international society.

We come finally to nationalism. How has the national idea influenced the evolution of international society. While the influence of nationalism has been enormously extensive, touching, at some point, most aspects of international life, the modern history of international society is neither subsumed within, nor exhausted by, the history of nationalism. The idea crystallised before the nationalist era, and its subsequent evolution has been influenced by ideas which are, at least, partially independent of the national idea. The principles of the Enlightenment were originally conceived in a universal, not a national, form. Similarly, the idea of a complex international division of labour serving a world market, was a response to the logic of industrial capitalism rather than to nationalism. Such ideas have led to efforts to create international standards and to establish structures for international cooperation.

Yet, despite the influence of these and other ideas, my argument is that the modification of the traditional conception of international society arose primarily from its confrontation with the national idea. In support of this claim let us review three themes which run through the book. These deal respectively with the national principle of international legitimacy; the way in which national identity is taken for granted in liberal (and for that matter socialist) ideology; and the national basis of political organisation in the modern state.

The most important impact has undoubtedly been the substitution of a popular for the prescriptive principle of sovereignty on which the original conception of international society was based. Conceivably, a principle of popular sovereignty could have been advanced without

149

tying it to the nation – it could have been expressed, for example, by a common imperial citizenship. However, the way in which the principles of the French Revolution were exported by Napoleon ensured that this did not happen in Europe. And the policies of the liberal imperialist powers in Asia and Africa ensured that it would not happen there also. The concept of a people was tied historically to the concept of nation, even where national consciousness was embryonic or even non-existent.

Once the principle of national self-determination had done its work in extinguishing the concept of empire as an acceptable political form, its continuing function in international society became largely mythic. Nations were deemed to have created states in their own image. No further creations were in order. Domestication of the concept has allowed it to support the sovereignty of existing states rather than subvert it. However, it still has enormous subversive appeal to all those actual and potential secessionists who remain convinced that their fundamental rights have been denied.

It is difficult to see the lineaments of some more satisfactory principle of state legitimisation emerging in the future. If government is to belong to the people (and to whom else?) then it cannot belong to mankind, which is, from an organisational point of view, a mere abstraction. Since communities do not exist within natural boundaries, there seems little alternative but to define the principle of popular sovereignty by reference to historical communities, or those whose collective identity is being created within frontiers handed down to them in the more recent past. Certainly the strength of national sentiment should not be underestimated. The Soviet Union, one of the few major states whose government claims to derive its legitimacy from an alternative source to the nation, has found that *perestroika*, the process of domestic reform, has revived national political demands in the Baltic republics and in the trans-Caucasus. Even limited schemes of liberal integration such as the United States–Canada Free Trade Agreement may be perceived by their opponents as an unwarranted attack on national identity. This does not mean that the national idea must frustrate all schemes for international cooperation, merely that those which ignore it, or confront it directly, are likely to meet with heavy and sustained resistance. The subversive appeal of national self-determination is not confined to third world secessionists.

In origin the idea of self-determination (i.e. the free development of individual potential) is impeccably liberal. Liberal thought is generally conceived of in terms of its opposition to nationalism. On this view, liberalism places the individual at the centre of the argument, nationalism the collective. The idea of national self-determination is not logically derived from the idea of an autonomous individual, it is a perversion of it. On one level this view is obviously correct. The argument of this book, however, is that this traditional opposition conceals the extent to which liberal international theory was explicitly statist and implicitly nationalist. This second theme was explored mainly with reference to the economic aspects of sovereignty, since national liberalism most clearly revealed itself in this area. The explicit statism stemmed from those legitimate state functions (defence, the maintenance of law and order and the stability of the currency) which liberal theorists reserved from their attack on the mercantilist system. The implicit nationalism derived partly from their acceptance of existing cultural communities as effectively 'natural' (and, therefore, invisible) and partly from the refinement of their argument to accommodate the principle of popular sovereignty. Liberal nationalism broke into the open after 1945 with the elaboration of the idea of the welfare state.

Not all nationalists are liberals. Indeed, in the popular imagination, the typical nationalist is likely to be portrayed as a romantic enthusiast, fundamentally opposed to the bloodless cosmopolitanism of liberal rationality. During the twentieth century the cult of national irrationalism has repeatedly savaged the liberal conception of international society, most infamously in the Nazi onslaught, but also more recently in Kampuchea and in innumerable communal massacres. These only appear to be less terrible because, from the outside, they seem to lack the purposeless, pre-meditated anti-morality of the holocaust.

After 1945 a deliberate attempt was made to create an international framework of political and economic cooperation which would channel the irrational and destructive potential of the national idea into a relatively benign liberal mould. This effort has not been wholly successful. It was, no doubt, compromised from the start by the cultural myopia of the victors of the Second World War, and the age-old tendency of the powerful to behave arrogantly towards the weak. But it created more possibilities for international cooperation and conflict resolution than had ever previously existed.

Ultimately, international society is an historical not a theoretical construct. Its moral order is neither functionally built-in nor guaranteed by the rationality of human nature. If the argument of this book is accepted, therefore, we should not look for our salvation to some miraculous or mechanical supersession of the national idea. The final theme is that nationalism has become structurally embodied, in all parts of the world, as the basis of the modern state. The implication is not that the nation-state is an eternal category or that some less deadly basis of political organisation and international solidarity may eventually emerge. It is that there is little sensible that we can say about these possibilities: on this issue, if no other, we lack a reliable guide to the future.

The nation-state (or the would-be nation-state) remains the basic political unit. It continues to define the primary space in which political argument takes place. The competing ideas, of a world market dominated by multi-national corporations to whom we owe loyalty, or international proletarian solidarity, are equally implausible. In relation to other states and peoples the nation-state also defines the context in which real, as opposed to fantastical, moral choices must be faced. We must live in the world we have made. Our task is not god-like: we cannot hope to transform the world, if we are very lucky we might just improve it.

NOTES

INTRODUCTION

1 Hedley Bull, *The Anarchical Society: A Study of Order in World Politics* (London, Macmillan, 1977), pp. 9–13.
2 See Peter Wilson, 'The English School of International Relations: a reply to Sheila Grader', *Review of International Studies*, vol. 15, no. 1, January 1989, pp. 49–58.
3 See Hugh Seton-Watson, *Nations and States: An Enquiry into the Origins of Nations and the Politics of Nationalism* (London, Methuen, 1977). Also note 2, chapter 1 below.

1 THE SEARCH FOR THE INTERNATIONAL SYSTEM: THE PROBLEM OF THEORY

1 F. H. Hinsley, *Nationalism and the International System* (London, Hodder and Stoughton, 1973) is the one serious attempt to bridge the gap.
2 The literature on nationalism within the three disciplines is extensive. A. D. Smith, *Theories of Nationalism* (London, Duckworth, 1971) provides an excellent introduction to the sociological literature. Alfred Cobban, *Nationalism and National Self-Determination* (London, Oxford University Press, 1969) is still the best historical introduction to the impact of nationalist ideas on international relations. Ernest Gellner, *Nations and Nationalism* (Oxford, Blackwell, 1983), Benedict Anderson, *Imagined Communities* (London, Verso, 1983) and John Breuilly, *Nationalism and the State* (Manchester, Manchester University Press, 1982) are amongst the most interesting recent additions to the literature.
3 Hobbes acknowledged his own debt to Thucydides and translated his *History of the Peloponnesian War*. See Michael Walzer, *Just and Unjust Wars* (London, Allen Lane, 1977), pp. 4–5.
4 Thomas Hobbes, *Leviathan*, edited with an introduction by Michael Oakshott (Oxford, Blackwell, 1927), p. 83.
5 David Hume, *Enquiries Concerning the Human Understanding and Concerning the Principles of Morals*, ed. by L. A. Selby-Bigge (Oxford, Clarendon Press, 1927), p. 190.
6 Hugo Grotius, *De Jure Belli Ac Pacis Libri Tres*, Prolegomena 11. Text printed in M. G. Forsyth, H. M. A. Keens-Soper and P. Savigear (eds.), *The Theory of International Relations* (London, Allen and Unwin, 1970), p. 45.
7 See the discussion of Durkheim's *Les Formes élémentaires de la vie religieuse* in

Raymond Aron, *Main Currents in Sociological Thought*, vol. 2 (London, Penguin, 1970), pp. 56–68.

8 Ernest Gellner, 'How to live in anarchy', in *Contemporary Thought and Politics*, ed. by I. C. Jarvie and Joseph Agassi (London, Routledge and Kegan Paul, 1974), pp. 87–94.

9 Raymond Aron, *On War* (London, Secker and Warburg, 1986); also *Peace and War* (London, Weidenfeld and Nicolson, 1966), part 3, pp. 369–574.

10 Cf. Bull, *The Anarchical Society*, 59–65.

11 For a critical discussion of this kind of argument, see Barrie Paskins, 'A Community of Terror?' in James Mayall (ed.), *The Community of States* (London, Allen and Unwin, 1982), pp. 85–95

2 THE SOCIETY OF STATES

1 Maurice Keens-Soper, 'The practice of a states-system', in Michael Donelan, *The Reason of States* (London, Allen and Unwin, 1978), pp. 24–44 and Richard Langhorne, 'The development of international conferences 1648–1830', in *Studies in History and Politics 1981/82*, Quebec, Bishops University, 1982, pp. 61–91.

2 In recent times, Henry Kissinger has been the most prominent exponent of this view of the great powers' responsibilities. See, for example, his statement before the Subcommittee on African Affairs of the Senate Committee on Foreign Relations, 29 January 1976: 'Peace requires a sense of security which depends upon some form of equilibrium. That equilibrium is impossible unless the United States remains both strong and determined to use its strength when required ... Military aggression, direct or indirect, has frequently been successfully dealt with, but never in the absence of a local balance of forces. United States policy in Angola sought to help friends achieve this balance.' *Angola, Hearings before the Sub-Committee on African Affairs* (Washington, 1976), pp. 6–7.

3 See Geoffrey Best, *Humanity in Warfare* (London, Weidenfeld and Nicolson, 1980), ch. 5.

4 Paul Sieghart, *The Lawful Rights of Mankind: An Introduction to the International Legal Code of Human Rights* (Oxford, Oxford University Press, 1985), pp. 67–8.

5 See Martin Wight, 'The balance of power', in Herbert Butterfield and Martin Wight (eds.), *Diplomatic Investigations* (London, Allen and Unwin, 1966), pp. 149–75.

6 The dominance of the nation-state in modern politics is well treated from a variety of perspectives in Leonard Tivey (ed.), *The Nation-State, The Formation of Modern Politics* (Oxford, Martin Robertson, 1981).

7 J. S. Mill, *Utilitarianism, Liberty, Representative Government*, introduction by A. D. Lindsay (London, J. M. Dent, Everyman's Library, 1910, reprinted 1957), ch. 16.

8 Ibid.

9 Ingrid Detter de Lupis, *The Law of War* (Cambridge University Press, 1987), pp. 121–37.

10 *On War* was first published in 1832. The main arguments on the distinction between Absolute and Real War, and on war as an instrument of policy, are

contained in vol. 3, Book 8. For a useful introduction see, Roger Ashley (ed.), *A Short Guide to Clausewitz on War* (London, Weidenfeld and Nicolson, 1967).

11 For text see M. G. Forsyth *et al.*, *The Theory of International Relations*, pp. 200–44.

12 *Hegel's Philosophy of Right*, translated with notes by T. M. Knox (Oxford, Oxford University Press, 1979), part 3: Ethical Life, (iii) The State (c) World History. The crucial paragraphs are 350–1. 'It is the absolute right of the Idea to step into existence in clear cut laws and objective institutions . . . whether this right be actualised in the form of divine legislation, or in the form of force and wrong. This right is the right of heroes to found states.

The same consideration justifies civilised nations in regarding and treating as barbarians those who lag behind them in institutions which are the essential moments of the State . . . the civilised nation is conscious that the rights of barbarians are unequal to its own and treats their autonomy as only a formality.

When wars and disputes arise in such circumstances, the trait which gives them a significance for world history is the fact that they are *struggles for recognition in connection with something of specific intrinsic worth*' (my italics).

13 The most sustained attack by a contemporary liberal on 'the legalist paradigm' is Walzer, *Just and Unjust Wars*, particularly chs. 4 and 6.

14 In justification of India's annexation of Goa, Krishna Menon, the Defence Minister, said: 'We consider colonialism is permanent aggression. We did not commit aggression. Colonialism collapsed.' *New York Times*, 20 December 1961. For an elaboration of the Indian position, see the statement before the Security Council by the Indian permanent representative, C. S. Jha on 18 December 1961. United Nations, *Security Council Official Records 987*, pp. 10–11.

15 It took two years for President de Gaulle to accept that the transfer of power had to be negotiated with the Algerian Government in Exile and its military arm, the FLN. With the benefit of hindsight, it is difficult to avoid the conclusion that his final decision was embedded in the initiative he announced at his first press conference after taking power, on 28 October 1958: 'The majority of insurgents have fought courageously. Let there be a peace of the brave, and I am sure that the hatred will die away . . .' *Keesings Contemporary Archives*, 28 November – 5 December 1959, col. 17129.

3 NATIONALISM AND THE CREATION OF STATES

1 John Locke, 'Of property', in *The Second Treatise of Government*, ch. 5.

2 J. S. Mill, 'Of property', *Principles of Political Economy*, book 2, ch. 1.

3 In western political thought this view ultimately presupposes that 'the ground in which the right-bestowing value is rooted is the individual himself', although the presupposition is not reflected in the UN Charter or other international documents, presumably because many of its supporters have wished to assert the priority of the national group as the source of the right to independence. Cf. John Charvet, *A Critique of Freedom and Equality* (Cambridge, Cambridge University Press, 1981), p. 12.

4 Smith, *Theories of Nationalism*, pp. 153–67.
5 José Ortega y Gasset, *The Revolt of the Masses*, authorised translation from the Spanish (London, Allen and Unwin, 1932), pp. 224–5.
6 The first draft of this chapter was written in the United States, often to the accompaniment of the afternoon radio news programme, 'All things considered'. Many women who were interviewed on the programme expressed their excitement at the Ferraro candidacy, others their deep apprehension at the apparent assault on the 'natural' order.
7 Mill, *Representative Government*.
8 W. I. Jennings, *The Approach to Self-Government* (Cambridge, Cambridge University Press, 1956), p. 56.
9 W. B. Gallie, *Philosophy and the Historical Understanding* (London, Chatto and Windus, 1964), ch. 8. Also Ernest Gellner, 'The concept of a story', in *Contemporary Thought and Politics*, pp. 95–111.
10 Cf. John Plamenatz, *On Alien Rule and Self-Government* (London, Longmans, 1960), ch. 1.
11 Benedetto Croce, *History as the Story of Liberty* (New York, Meridian Books, 1955), p. 57.
12 See Geoffrey Best (ed.), *The Permanent Revolution: The French Revolution and its Legacy, 1789–1989* (London, Fontana, 1988), particularly the chapter on nationalism by Conor Cruise O'Brien.
13 Cf. W. J. Argyle, 'European Nationalism and African Tribalism', in P. H. Gulliver (ed.), *Tradition and Transition in East Africa* (London, Routledge and Kegan Paul, 1969), pp. 41–57.
14 Mill, *Representative Government*, ch. 16.
15 Alfred Cobban, *National Self-Determination* (London, Oxford University Press for the Royal Institute of International Affairs, 1945), p. 26.
16 Ibid. ch. 3. See also J. M. Keynes, *Essays in Biography* (London, Macmillan, 1933) for a brilliant and caustic assessment of the major protagonists by one of those present at the Versailles Conference.
17 I have discussed the non-availability of the 'barbarian option' more fully in 'International society and international theory', in Donelan (ed.), *The Reason of States*, pp. 122–41. See also Hedley Bull and Adam Watson (eds.), *The Expansion of International Society* (Oxford, Clarendon Press, 1984), ch. 8.
18 Elie Kedourie, *Nationalism in Asia and Africa* (New York, The World Publishing Co., 1970), Introduction.
19 Cf. Wm. Roger Louis, 'The era of the mandates system and the non-European world', in Bull and Watson, *The Expansion of International Society*, pp. 201–13.
20 Dov Ronen, *The Quest for Self-Determination* (New Haven and London, Yale University Press, 1979), p. 52.
21 Declaration on the Granting of Independence to Colonial Countries and Peoples: UN General Assembly Resolution 1514 (XV). Text in Ian Brownlie (ed.), *Basic Documents on African Affairs* (Oxford, Clarendon Press, 1971), pp. 365–8.

4 NATIONALISM AND THE INTERNATIONAL ORDER
1 Mill, *Representative Government*, ch. 16.

2 In a discussion of the principle of majority rule, Harry Beran has devised a system of 'reiterated plebiscites' in which the group to be polled defines itself, and then dissatisfied minorities within the territory can opt out through further plebiscites. The proposal is designed to overcome the theoretical objections to the plebiscite. It is too early to say, under what circumstances, this ingenious scheme might recommend itself to governments. Harry Beran, *The Consent Theory of Political Obligation* (London, Croom Helm, 1987), pp. 39–42.

3 Cobban, *National Self-Determination*, p. 26.

4 There is a vast literature on the Kashmir dispute. For a balanced account by an Indian author see Sisir Gupta, *Kashmir – A Study in India–Pakistan Relations* (London, Asia Publishing House, 1966) and, for a useful survey of the view from Pakistan, G. W. Choudhury, *Pakistan's Relation with India 1947–66* (London, Pall Mall Press, 1968).

5 Cobban, *National Self-Determination*, pp. 53–4.

6 Ibid., pp. 27–8.

7 Martin Wight, *Systems of States* (Leicester, Leicester University Press, 1977), ch. 6, p. 167.

8. Ibid.

9 Sally Healy, 'The changing idiom of self-determination in the Horn of Africa', and James Mayall, 'Self-determination and the OAU', in I. M. Lewis (ed.), *Nationalism and Self-Determination in the Horn of Africa* (London, Ithica Press, 1983), pp. 77–110.

10 See, for example, M. Honeywell, J. Pearce *et al.*, *Falklands–Malvenas: Whose Crisis?* (London, Latin American Bureau, 1982) and *Millennium: Journal of International Studies*, special issue,*The Falklands Crisis: One Year Later*, vol. 12, no. 1, 1983.

11 Anthony S. Rayner, 'Morocco's international boundaries: a factual background', *Journal of Modern African Studies*, vol. 1, no. 3, 1963; Edouard Meric, 'Le Conflit Algero-Marocain', *Revue Française de Science Politique*, vol. 15, no. 4, 1965; also Patricia Berko Wild, 'The Organisation of African Unity and the Algerian–Moroccan border conflict', *International Organisation*, vol. 20, no. 1, 19.

12 Witness the difficulty which, in early 1985, the British and Spanish governments had in arriving at a formula which would allow the reopening of the border between Gibraltar and Spain without prejudicing possible future negotiations on the issue of sovereignty; and the difficulties of the British and Irish governments in finding a stable basis on which to discuss the Northern Irish problem.

13 See John Drysdale, *The Somali Dispute* (London, Pall Mall Press, 1964) and I. M. Lewis, *A Modern History of Somalia* (London, Longmans, 1980).

14 Vincent Thompson, 'Conflict in the Horn of Africa: a study of the Kenya–Somalia border problem, 1941–1948' (University of London, PhD thesis, 1985).

15 Alistair Lamb, *The China–Indian Border: The Origins of the Disputed Boundaries* (London, Oxford University Press, 1964), ch. 3.

16 M. D. Donelan and M. J. Grieve, *International Disputes: Case Histories 1945–1970* (London, Europa Publications, 1973) pp. 147–50.

17 The International Court of Justice was asked firstly, whether Western Sahara was a territory belonging to no-one at the time of its colonisation and secondly, if not, what legal ties existed between the territory, the kingdom or Morocco and the 'Mauritanian Entity'. Its opinion was delivered on 16 October 1975. On the first count, by a vote of 13–3, the Court judged that the territory did not belong to anyone; on the second, by votes of 14–2 and 15–2 respectively, it found that only limited legal ties existed between the territory and the kingdom of Morocco and Mauritania. The substantive passage of the opinion reads as follows: 'The Court's conclusion is that the material and information presented to it do not establish any tie of territorial sovereignty between the territory of western Sahara and the kingdom Morocco. Thus the Court has not found legal ties of such a nature as might affect the application of General Assembly Resolution 1514 (XV) on the decolonisation of Western Sahara and, in particular, of the expression of self-determination through the free and genuine expression of the will of the peoples of the territory.'

18 Gellner, *Nations and Nationalism*, pp. 43–50.

19 On 10 July 1973 the Pakistan National Assembly passed a unanimous resolution authorising President Bhutto to recognise Bangladesh 'at the appropriate time'. Diplomatic recognition was finally announced shortly before the opening of the Islamic Conference on 22 February 1974.

20 Selig F. Harrison, *In Afghanistan's Shadow: Baluch Nationalism and Soviet Temptation* (New York, Carnegie Endowment for International Peace, 1981), ch. 7.

21 L. C. Buchheit, *Secession, The Legitimacy of Self-Determination* (New Haven and London, Yale University Press, 1978), p. 119.

22 Ibid. pp. 98–9.

23 Ian Lustick, *State-building in British Ireland and French Algeria* (Berkeley, Institute of International Studies, University of California, 1985), pp. 17–39, and 45.

24 A. D. Smith, *The Ethnic Revival in the Modern World* (Cambridge, Cambridge University Press, 1981), ch. 9.

5 ECONOMIC NATIONALISM AND THE LIBERAL WORLD ORDER

1 For an account of the contending explanations see A. D. Smith, *Theories of Nationalism*.

2 On the influence of mercantilist thought on economic statecraft see David Baldwin, *Economic Statecraft* (Princeton, Princeton University Press, 1985), pp. 72–6; and for an assessment of mercantilist doctrines themselves, D. C. Coleman (ed.), *Revisions in Mercantilism* (London, Methuen, 1969).

3 Jacob Viner, 'Power versus plenty as objectives of foreign policy in the seventeenth and eighteenth centuries', *World Politics*, vol. 1, no. 1, 1948, pp. 1–29.

4 'Perpetual combat in peace and war among the nations of Europe as to which will gain the upper hand'. cited by E. Silberner, *La Guerre dans la pensée Economique du XVIe au XVIIIe Siècle* (Paris, Librairie du Recueil Sirey, 1939), p. 35.

5 'It is only the abundance of money in a state that makes the difference as to its greatness and its power.' Ibid., p. 34.

6 Aron, *Peace and War*, p. 245.
7 In Smith's case it was only the economic policies of the *Ancien Régime* which were attacked, not the principle of prescriptive sovereignty.
8 Felix Gilbert, 'The new diplomacy of the eighteenth century', *World Politics*, vol. 4, no. 1, 1951, pp. 1–38.
9 'All pacifism not based on a liberal economic order built on private ownership of the means of production always remains utopian. Whoever wants peace among nations must seek to limit the state and its influence most strictly.' Ludwig von Mises, *Nation, State and Economy: Contributions to the Politics and History of Our Time*, translated by Leland B. Yeager (New York, New York University Press, 1983), p. 94. This book, originally published in 1919, contains a passionate defence of liberalism within a nationalist and imperialist world.
10 Adam Smith, *Wealth of Nations*, book 4, ch. 2, para. 30.
11 Joseph Cropsey, *Political Philosophy and the Issues of Politics* (Chicago and London, University of Chicago Press, 1977), p. 78.
12 'It is quite as important to the happiness of mankind, that our enjoyments should be increased by the better distribution of labour, by each country producing those commodities for which by its situation, its climate, and its other natural or artificial advantages, it is adapted, and by then exchanging them for the commodities of other countries, as that they should be augmented by a rise in the rate of profits.' P. Straffa (ed.), *The Works of David Ricardo* (Cambridge, Cambridge University Press, 1951), vol. 1, *The Principles of Political Economy*, ch. 7, p. 132.
13 See Karl Polanyi, *The Great Transformation: Origins of our Time* (Boston, Beacon Press, 1957).
14 Violet Barbour, *Capitalism in Amsterdam in the Seventeenth Century* (Ann Arbor, University of Michigan Press, 1966), p. 130, cited in Charles P. Kindleberger, *Government and International Trade* (Princeton Essays in International Finance, no. 129, July 1978), p. 14.
15 The early liberal economists were much more practical and empirical in their approach than this formulation suggests. Indeed the theory of free trade was originally developed on the assumption that while goods could move freely capital and labour would stay at home.
16 Gerrard Curzon, *Multilateral Commercial Diplomacy* (London, Michael Joseph, 1965), ch. 3.
17 Eric Roll, *A History of Economic Thought* (London, Faber, 1961), p. 226.
18 Johann Gottlieb Fichte, *Der Geschlossne Handelsstaat* (Tubingen, 1800, republished by the Gustav Fischer Verlag in Jena, 1920). For an extended English treatment of the closed commercial state which includes extensive translated extracts from the 1920 Jena edition, see Michael A. Heilprin, *Studies in Economic Nationalism* (Geneva, Librairie E. Droz; Paris, Librairie Minard, 1960), ch. 5.
19 Albert O. Hirschman, *National Power and the Structure of Foreign Trade* (Berkeley and Los Angeles, University of California Press, 1945), pp. 34–40.
20 R. F. Alfred Hoernle, *South African Native Policy and the Liberal Spirit* (Johannesburg, Witwatersrand University Press, 1945); Edgar H. Brookes,

The History of Native Policy in South Africa (Capetown, Nasionale Pers, 1924).

21 W. A. de Klerk, *The Puritans in Africa, A Story of Afrikanerdom* (London, Rex Collins, 1975), pp. 22–7.

22 Changes in political conditions, and business confidence, may undermine the plausibility of this argument. Since the urban revolt in 1984 the South African government has maintained control by imposing a State of Emergency and using the military to police the African townships. However, external confidence in the long-run viability of the state appears to have been undermined and the government has found it impossible to attract new capital from abroad.

23 Friedrich List, *The National System of Political Economy*, translated by Sampson S. Lloyd (London, Longmans Green and Co., 1885).

24 Dudley Seers, *The Political Economy of Nationalism* (Oxford, Oxford University Press, 1983), p. 52.

6 THE NEW ECONOMIC NATIONALISM

1 J. M. Keynes, 'National self-sufficiency', *Yale Review*, vol. 22, 1934, pp. 755–69.

2 Richard N. Gardner, *Sterling–Dollar Diplomacy* (London, Oxford University Press, 1956; republished with a new introduction, New York, Columbia University Press, 1980).

3 See Charles P. Kindelberger, *The World in Depression 1929–39* (Berkeley, University of California Press, 1973); Mancur Olson, *The Rise and Decline of Nations* (New Haven and London, Yale University Press, 1982); Robert O. Keohane, *After Hegemony* (Princeton, Princeton University Press, 1984); Robert Gilpin, *The Political Economy of International Relations* (Princeton, Princeton University Press, 1987); Arthur A. Stein, 'The hegemons dilemma: Great Britain, the United States, and the international economic order', *International Organisation*, vol. 38, no. 2, Spring 1984, pp. 355–86; Susan Strange, 'The persistant myth of lost hegemony', *International Organisation*, vol. 41, no. 4, Autumn 1984, pp. 551–74.

4 Jeremy Morse, 'The dollar as a reserve currency', *International Affairs*, July 1979, pp. 359–66.

5 Jacob Viner, *The Customs Union Issue* (New York, Carnegie Endowment for International Peace, 1950); Sydney S. Bell, *Trade Blocks and Common Markets* (London, Constable, 1963).

6 For a good comparative account, the conclusions of which remain largely valid, see Roger D. Hansen, 'Regional integration, reflections on a decade of theoretical efforts', *World Politics*, vol. 21, January 1969, pp. 242–71.

7 I have developed the argument of this section in more detail in, 'Reflections on the "new" economic nationalism', *Review of International Studies*, vol. 10, no. 4, October 1984, pp. 311–21.

8 I have discussed the problems of incorporating the Eastern trading area in the international economic order in 'East–West trade, GATT and the Western Alliance', in David Baldwin and Helen Milner (eds.), *East–West Trade and the Western Alliance* (New York, St Martin's Press, forthcoming).

9 Mill, *Principles of Political Economy*, ch. 11.

10 In Britain the physical deterioration of the population became a matter of

urgent public concern during the Boer War when 'less than 10 per cent of the volunteers were considered fit enough to send abroad to fight', Anthony S. Wohl, *Endangered Lives: Public Health in Victorian Britain* (London, Methuen, 1984), pp. 332–3.

11 Richard Cooper, *The Economics of Interdependence: Economic Policy in the Atlantic Community* (New York, McGraw-Hill, 1968); Miriam Camps, *The Management of Interdependence: A Preliminary View* (New York, Council on Foreign Relations, 1974).

12 Ebba Dohlman, *National Welfare and Economic Interdependence: The Case of Sweden's Foreign Trade Policy* (London, Oxford University Press, 1989).

13 Susan Strange, 'The new protectionism', *International Organisation*, vol. 39, no. 2, Spring 1985, pp. 233–60.

14 On the relationship of Keynes's theory and his pragmatism, see Robert Heilbronner, *The Worldly Philosophers* (New York, Simon and Schuster, 1980), ch. 9; and Joan Robinson, *Economic Philosophy* (London, Penguin Books, 1962), ch. 4.

15 The relatively strong 'predisposition to consensus' by German and Austrian unionists has been explained as the result of a 'unique historical experience that imposed itself strongly on the national consciousness: the hyper inflation of the 1920s and the tragic political events that followed it. It was also rooted in a traditional acceptance of the function of government in providing for economic security of the individual and the obligation of private interest groups to exercise restraint in the national public interest.' Robert J. Flanagan, David W. Soskice, Lloyd Ulman, *Unionism, Economic Stabilization and Incomes Policies, European Experience* (Washington, DC, The Brookings Institution, 1983), p. 687.

16 Louis and Bull (eds.), *The Special Relationship*, chs. 2, 11 and 16.

17 In 1972 the United States was 69 per cent self-sufficient in oil production compared with 3 per cent and zero for Western Europe and Japan respectively. Philip Connelly and Robert Perlman, *The Politics of Scarcity: Resource Conflicts in International Relations* (London, Oxford University Press for the RIIA, 1975), p. 98.

18 Dan Smith, 'Long term contracts for the supply of raw materials', in Sir John Crawford and Saburo Okita (eds.), *Raw Materials and Pacific Economic Integration* (London, Croom Helm, 1978), pp. 229–70.

19 Geoffrey Goodwin and James Mayall (eds.), *A New International Commodity Regime* (London, Croom Helm, 1979), p. 21.

20 See Robert Middleton, *Negotiating on Non-Tariff Distortions of Trade: The EFTA Precedents* (New York, St Martins Press, 1985).

21 S. J. Warnecke (ed.), *International Trade and Industrial Subsidy Policies* (London, Holmes and Meier, 1978).

22 Cf. Ernest Gellner, *Plough, Sword and Book: The Structure of Human History* (London, Collins, Harvill, 1988), pp. 264–5.

23 On the relationship between the civil and military economies, see Barry Buzan and Gautam Sen, *The Impact of Military Research and Development Priorities on the Evolution of the Civil Economy in Capitalist States* (CEPR Workshop paper on 'Economic Aspects of International Security', 12 February 1988, Chatham House).

7 POST-COLONIAL NATIONALISM

1 For example, 'The de-Westernisation or de-establishment of the short-lived global international order constitutes a major challenge to European and American diplomacy ... occidental diplomacy must henceforth be prepared to function again, as it did before the nineteenth century, in a world that has no common culture and no overarching political order, and that is no longer prepared to abide by Western standards of international conduct', Adda Bozeman, 'The international order in a multicultural world', in Bull and Watson (eds.), *The Expansion of International Society*, p. 406. See also Bozeman, *The Future of Law in a Multicultural World* (Princeton, Princeton University Press, 1971), pp. 161–86, and Elie Kedourie, 'A new international disorder', in Bull and Watson, *The Expansion of International Society*, pp. 347–55. I have presented an argument opposed to these positions in 'International society and international theory', in Donelan (ed.), *The Reason of States*, pp. 122–41.

2 For an original and highly suggestive treatment of this theme see William Bloom, 'National Identity in International Relations, Personal Identity, Political Integration and Mass Mobilisation' (University of London, PhD, 1987).

3 Hugh Seton-Watson, *Nations and States* (London, Methuen, 1977), chs. 6, 7 and 8.

4 On the influence of Marxism–Leninism on Asia, see Hélène Carrère d'Encausse and Stuart R. Schram, *Marxism and Asia: An Introduction with Readings* (London, Allen Lane, 1965), and on Africa, Zbigniew Brzezinsky (ed.), *Africa and the Communist World* (Stanford, Stanford University Press, 1963), ch. 1.

5 Marx's views on the national question are scattered through his writings. They may be distilled, *inter alia*, from the 'Manifesto of the Communist Party', the 'Class Struggles in France', and his newspaper articles on British rule in India, all reprinted in *Karl Marx and Frederick Engels, Selected Works, Vol. I* (Moscow, Foreign Language Publishing House, 1958). For his views supporting the Polish and Irish struggles for national independence see d'Encausse and Schram, *Marxism and Asia*, pp. 121–2. Also, Erica L. Benner, 'Marx and Engels on nationalism and national identity: a reappraisal', *Millennium*, vol. 17, no. 1, Spring 1988, pp. 1023, and Margot Light, *The Soviet Theory of International Relations* (New York, St Martin's Press, 1988), ch. 4.

6 Cf. the open letter written by Aime Cesaire to Maurice Thorez, the Secretary-General of the French Communist Party in 1956: 'what I want is that Marxism and Communism be harnessed into the service of coloured people, and not coloured people into the service of Marxism and Communism'. (Paris, *Presence Africaine*, 1956), p. 12, cited in Waldemar A. Nielson, *The Great Powers and Africa* (London, Pall Mall, 1969), p. 189.

7 Richard Loewenthal, *Model or Ally? The Communist Powers and the Developing Countries* (New York, Oxford University Press, 1977), pp. 184–5.

8 Louis and Bull, *The Special Relationship*, pp. 32–3.

9 Ernest Gellner, 'Recollection in anxiety: *Thought and Change* revisited', in *Culture, Identity and Politics* (Cambridge, Cambridge University Press, 1987), pp. 111–22.

10 On non-alignment see Peter Lyon, *Neutralism* (Leicester, Leicester University Press, 1963); Leo Mates, *Non-alignment: Theory and Current Policy* (New York and Belgrade, Oceana Publications Inc., 1972).

11 See Lawrence W. Martin (ed.), *Neutralism and Non-Alignment* (New York, Praeger, 1962), chs. 4 and 5.

12 The concept of 'national democracy' was formerly introduced and defined in the Statement of Eighty-One Communist Parties adopted in December 1960. For text see D'Encausse and Schram, *Marxism and Asia*, pp. 306-9.

13 On Soviet and western views of development aid in India, see P. J. Eldridge, *The Politics of Foreign Aid in India* (London, Weidenfeld and Nicolson, 1969) and Stephen Clarkson, *The Soviet Theory of Development: India and the Third World in Marxist Leninist Scholarship* (Toronto, University of Toronto Press, 1978), pp. 164-82.

14 Stephen D. Krasner, *Structural Conflict: The Third World Against Global Liberalism* (Berkeley, University of California Press, 1985), p. 95.

15 Ernest Gellner, 'A social contract in search of an idiom: the demise of the Danegeld state', in *Spectacles and Predicaments: Essays in Social Theory* (Cambridge, Cambridge University Press, 1979), pp. 207-306.

16 Mill argues, for example, that 'under despotic rule identity of situation often produces harmony of feeling and the different races come to feel towards each other as fellow common men; particularly if they are disposed over the same tract of country. But if the era of aspiration to free government arrives before this fusion has been effected, the opportunity has gone for effecting it.' *Representative Government*, ch. 16.

17 See Gautam Sen, *The Military Origins of Industrialization and International Trade Rivalry* (London, Frances Pinter, 1984).

18 The best known American blueprint is W. W. Rostow, *The Stages of Economic Growth: A Non-Communist Manifesto* (Cambridge, Cambridge University Press, 1960). For the Soviet Union, see Loewenthal, *Model or Ally? The Communist Powers and the Developing Countries*.

19 Robert Jackson, 'Negative sovereignty in Sub-Saharan Africa', *Review of International Studies*, vol. 12, October, 1986, pp. 247-64, and 'Quasi-states, dual regimes and neo-classical theory: international jurisprudence and the Third World', *International Organisation*, vol. 41, no. 4, Autumn 1987, pp. 519-50.

20 Ali Mazrui, *Africa's International Relations: the diplomacy of dependence and change* (London, Heinemann; Boulder, Westview Press, 1977), p. 240.

21 The range of ethnic and separatist groups in South Asia is well described in Urmila Phadnis, 'Ethnic tensions in South Asia - implications for regional cooperation', in Bhabani Sen Gupta (ed.), *Regional Cooperation and Development in South Asia*, vol. 2. *Political, Social, Technological and Research Aspects* (New Delhi, South Asia Publishers, 1987), pp. 1-5.

8 THE THIRD WORLD AND INTERNATIONAL SOCIETY

1 For an account of the evolution of the term, see Leslie Wolf-Phillips, 'Why "third world"?: origin, definition and usage', *Third World Quarterly*, vol. 9, no. 4, October 1987, pp. 1311-27.

2 Shiva Naipaul, 'The myth of the third world: a thousand million invisible men', *The Spectator*, 18 May 1985.

3 Third world leaders are not alone in viewing the alliance in this light, although they generally see a problem in what many western observers regard as a solution. Writing on 'NATO's middle course' for the American journal *Foreign Policy*, Winter 1987–8, David Calleo described the organisation as embodying 'the geo-political coalition between the United States and Western Europe that has contained the Soviet Union on its home ground and given America a wide margin of power to shape the world political and economic structures ... Thanks to NATO the twentieth century became the "American century" and much of the world has enjoyed a liberal and prosperous Pax Americana.'

4 Merle Lipton, *Capitalism and Apartheid* (London, Gower/Maurice Temple Smith, 1985), p. 295.

5 For an assessment of this literature see ibid., ch. 1, 'The debate about South Africa'.

6 Ethnic or communal nationalists are not necessarily separatists; where they have not been muzzled they may also attempt to arouse mass sentiment against the government at the state level. Consider the following example from the Indian weekly, *The Organiser*, which regularly contains material of this kind. The paper supports the policies of the BJP, the Hindu communal party. 'Yes, for too long have I suffered the affronts in silence ... My people have been kidnapped by the hostiles. My numbers have dwindled. As a result my adored motherland has been torn asunder. I have been deprived of my age old rights over my own hearths and homes. Afghanistan, NWFP, Sind, Baluchistan, half of Punjab, half of Bengal and a third of Kashmir – all these have been usurped from me. And subjugated to untold atrocities, dishonour and massacres. I was thrown out from there.' 'Angry Hindu! – yes: why not?', by an angry Hindu, *The Organiser*, 14 February 1988.

7 For a concise assessment of dependency theory, with particular reference to Latin America, see Ian Roxborough, *Theories of Underdevelopment* (London, Macmillan, 1979); also Dudley Seers (ed.), *Dependency Theory: A Critical Reassessment* (London, Frances Pinter, 1981).

8 Phadnis, 'Ethnic tensions in South Asia', in Gupta, *Regional Cooperation and Development in South Asia*, p. 10. See also A. W. Orridge, 'Uneven development and nationalism', *Political Studies*, vol. 29, no. 1, pp. 1–15 and no. 2, pp. 181–90.

9 The manifesto issued at the first congress of the Comintern in March 1919 declared that 'the liberation of the colonies is thinkable only in connexion with the liberation of the working class in the metropolitan countries ... Colonial slaves of Africa and Asia! The hour of the proletarian dictatorship in Europe will strike for you as the hour of your deliverance.' Cited in E. H. Carr, *The Bolshevik Revolution 1917–23* (London, Penguin Books, 1966), vol. 3, p. 238.

10 The attempt to extend welfare principles from the democratic state to international society underlies the work of the Brandt Commission. Recommendations 1 and 3 of the First Report, for example, call for the enlargement of official development finance by 'an international system of universal revenue mobilisation based on a sliding scale related to national

income in which Eastern Europe and Developing Countries – except the poorest – would participate', and by the 'introduction of automatic revenue transfers through international levies on ... international trade, arms production and exports; international travel; the global commons, especially seabed minerals', *North–South; A Programme for Survival* (London, Pan Books, 1980), p. 255. I have discussed the problems involved in this approach to international economic reform in the 'Liberal economy', in Mayall (ed.), *The Community of States*, pp. 96–111.

11 *Towards a New Trade Policy for Development; Report by the Secretary-General of the United Nations Conference on Trade and Development*, United Nations, E/CONF. 46/3, New York 1964.

12 Some contemporary writers on human rights have attempted to repair this omission in liberal theory. See, in particular, Henry Shue, *Basic Rights, Subsistence, Affluence and US Foreign Policy* (Princeton, Princeton University Press, 1980), and R. J.Vincent, *Human Rights and International Relations* (Cambridge, Cambridge University Press, for RIIA 1986), ch. 8.

13 For an assessment of the Third World Reform Movement in GATT see Diana Tussie, *The Less Developed Countries and the World Trading System; A Challenge to the GATT* (London, Frances Pinter, 1987), pp. 25–9.

14 Ibid.

15 Prebisch's analysis was supported by a number of other economists, most notably Hans Singer, *International Development: Growth and Change* (New York, McGraw Hill, 1964).

16 Robert L. Rothstein, *The Weak in the World of the Strong: The Developing Countries in the International System* (New York, Columbia University Press, 1977), pp. 136–59.

17 Ibid., pp. 79–86.

18 *Financing Africa's Recovery: Report and Recommendations of the Advisory Group on Financial Flows for Africa* (New York, United Nations, 1988).

19 See Krasner, *Structural Conflict: The Third World Against Global Liberalism*, pp. 81–92, and 104–10.

20 Goodwin and Mayall (eds.), *A New International Commodity Regime*, p. 128.

21 Ibid., pp. 71–6.

INDEX

166